ALSO BY PENELOPE LEACH

Your Growing Child: From Babyhood Through Adolescence (1984)

Your Baby & Child: From Birth to Age Five (1978)

Babyhood (1974, 1983)

THESE ARE BORZOI BOOKS
PUBLISHED IN NEW YORK
BY ALFRED A. KNOPF, INC.

The First Six Months

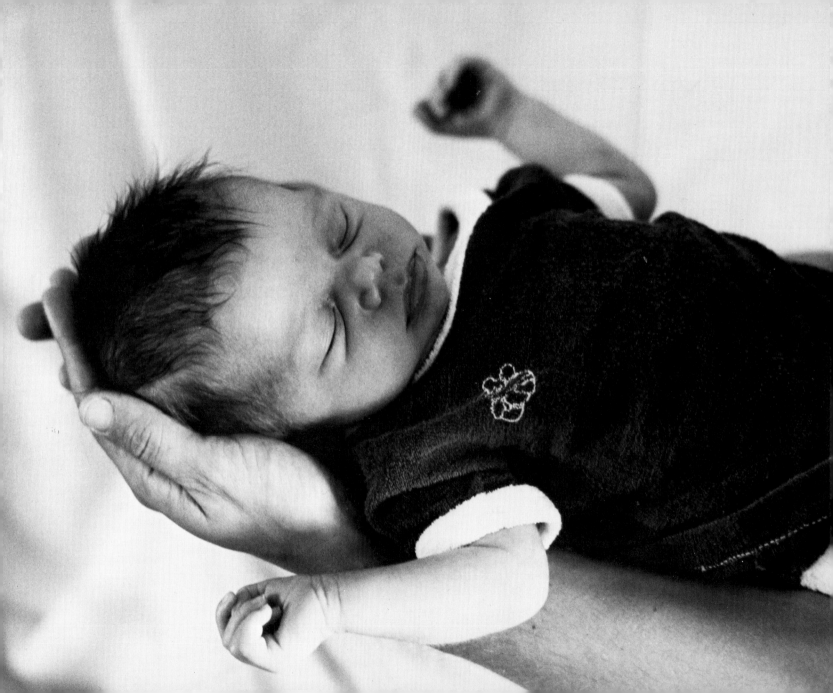

PENELOPE LEACH

The First Six Months

Getting together with your baby

Photographs by John Campbell

ALFRED A. KNOPF   New York   1987

To Alexander and Freja

who reminded me

THIS IS A BORZOI BOOK
PUBLISHED BY ALFRED A. KNOPF, INC.

Copyright © 1986, 1987 by Penelope Leach
Photographs copyright © 1986 by John Campbell
All rights reserved under International and Pan-American Copyright Conventions.
Published in the United States by Alfred A. Knopf, Inc., New York.
Distributed by Random House, Inc., New York.
Originally published, in different form, in Great Britain
by William Collins Sons & Co. Ltd, London.

Library of Congress Cataloging-in-Publication Data
Leach, Penelope.
The first six months.
1. Infants—Care and hygiene.
2. Infants—Care and hygiene—Psychological aspects.
3. Parent and child.
I. Title.   II. Title: First 6 months.
RJ61.L426   1987   649'.122   86–45304
ISBN 0–394–55375–6

Manufactured in the United States of America
First American Edition

Contents

Introduction 3

1 Becoming a family 7

2 Coming to terms with your newborn 21

3 Needs and wants 35

4 Meeting your new baby's needs: complications 45

5 Wallowing in early smiles 61

6 Tuning in to your baby as a person 69

7 If being tuned in only deafens you 85

8 Expanding your growing baby's world 93

9 Beginning to know that you are you 107

10 Beginning to take an active part in the world 115

11 The joys and sorrows of being half a year old 125

The First Six Months

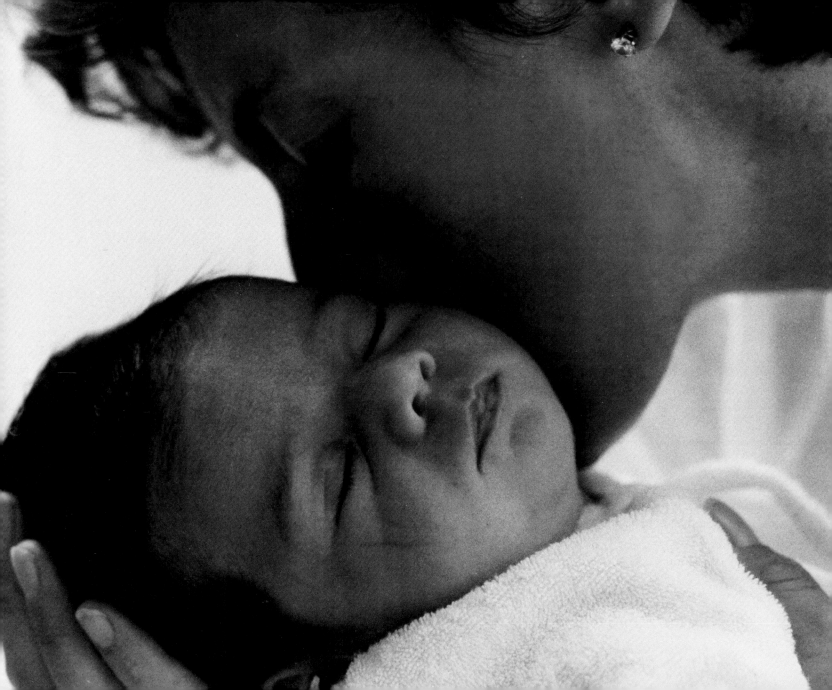

Introduction

Every time your clock ticks, two or three more people become parents somewhere in the world. The births of first children are not just everyday but every-second affairs, yet for every woman, and for many of their partners, a first birth is life's biggest landmark.

All those babies matter. They matter because they are new people. Whatever else a community or a society makes or cares about, it must make and care about new people if it is to continue. Western societies leave not only the making but also the caring almost entirely to individual parents. The job you do as a parent will matter to society because it will affect the kind of person your baby becomes, but the baby herself will seem to matter only to you. And she will matter more than anything else in the world.

Having a baby — especially a first baby — is always an anxious business because a minute, helpless, brand-new person is a tremendous responsibility and it feels heavy. You can carry it, though. You *can* rear a healthy, happy baby who becomes a cheerful, intelligent, reasonable child who eventually turns into an adult whom you really like. You will do it better and with greater pleasure if you do it wholeheartedly.

A baby is not a toy. You cannot put it away in a closet when you are tired of playing with it or when you need to do something else. Once your baby is outside your body, she will be ever-present. Everything and everybody else who is important to you will have to move over to make space

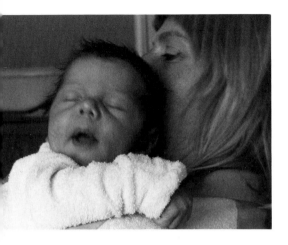

for her. Bringing up a baby is not a hobby, either. You cannot fit it in around the edges of an already full and fulfilling life. Your baby's care will be central.

Society will do little to help the two of you make that space at the center of your lives. Nobody will *offer* you the time and space and money that you need, and many will resent you taking it. Men-who-are-fathers are often forced to pretend that their babies *are* toys and that being a parent *is* a hobby. Their lives are dominated by paid jobs and, far from offering flexi-time or a bonus, employers offer overtime "now that you've got another mouth to feed."

Women-who-become-mothers cannot go on living as they lived before and should not even have to pretend to do so, to outsiders, to their partners, or to themselves. For a while — perhaps for three months, perhaps for two or three times longer — you will find that deep down inside you, nothing matters as much as your baby and nothing which is unimportant to your baby can be very important to you. You will not really be able to tell where "you" end and "the baby" begins because you will feel as if you and she were still part of each other. Even when you are physically away from her, leaving her minute-by-minute care to somebody else, invisible elastic threads will seem to join you together, pulling you back. You are your baby's other half; her protector, champion, and playmate. She is not designed to live without you in these first months. You know it even when nobody else will acknowledge it.

Many first-time mothers are amazed at the strength of their own feelings and every time outsiders suggest that the feelings are inappropriate, that amazement is tinged with alarm and dismay. Instead of saying "It's all right. You are *meant* to feel like this for a bit; your baby *needs* you to feel like this. Relax, accept it, revel in it," people suggest the very opposite. Nurses on the maternity floor say, "Now you have a nice nap, dear. Take advantage of being here. We'll look after baby." "Baby" is *your* baby and he is one hour old. You have only just got him. The very last thing you want is to have him taken away again so that a separate "you" can rest.

Your own mother says, "I hope you're not going to go on having her in the bedroom all night. She'd be much better off in her own room next door. . . ." She is six days old and she used to be inside you. If your now-separated bodies are to be cut off from each other in sleep, you want to trail your hand over the edge of her basket and know that her waking sounds are only two feet from your ear.

Sooner or later somebody will probably tell you that you are "turning into a cow," that you are "overprotective" or a "fussy mother." Try not to hear. If offering milk from your body to the baby that body made is being a cow, so be it. You will stop wanting to feed and comfort her in that particular way as and when she grows out of wanting you to. How could you be *over*protective of a baby who is still completely helpless and for whom you know you would kill or die? As for being "fussy": if that means trying to make your baby's new way of life as easy, comfortable, and perfect as you can, including telephoning doctors at midnight if necessary and asking forty-seven questions at the clinic, go to it. Nobody will fuss over your baby if you do not.

If you can believe that reveling in your baby is a highly desirable way to spend the next few months, you will be able to treat this period of your life as the unique experience it really is. Just have confidence that it will pass. However deeply you submerge yourself, you will not drown in babies and be lost to the adult world forever. Give yourselves a few months for each child you plan to have, and give yourselves freely and without rationing. It is very little time to take out of a whole adult life; whatever you lose by it, the gain to all of you will be infinitely greater.

1 Becoming a family

Once you have your baby, neither of you will ever be the same again. Birth preparation classes may have readied you for bodily upheavals and inevitable changes in your lifestyle, but nobody is likely to have suggested the total upheaval in feelings which is going to change you into different people.

Like it or not, you are going to be emotionally involved with this baby in a way you have never been involved before, and having this unique relationship of new parent to new child is going to change the way you think and feel about yourselves, each other, your own parents, your jobs, your community. . . .

Formal preparation for this vital aspect of becoming a family is impossible because you are unique individuals and, while it is safe to say that you are going to experience intense and far-reaching feelings, nobody can tell you what those feelings are going to feel like. You cannot even prepare yourselves entirely. You are both so used to the way you feel about things, as separate people and as a pair, that it is hard to imagine feeling differently. But if you know something about the emotional climate into which you are moving, you can at least think about it; be aware of things as they start to happen, and look for positive ways through or around them.

New parents who are taken completely off guard by the storm of emotions a new baby evokes often try to fight them down rather than work through them. They struggle to regain their past equilibrium and to convince themselves (and each other) that they are still the people they used to be, rather than search for a new balance, for people who are suddenly parents and a partnership which is suddenly a family.

Sitting on strong waves of feeling is seldom a good idea. If people will not allow themselves to feel, will not take out their emotions and have a good look at them, those feelings have a clever way of turning themselves inside out so as to sneak past defenses in a new guise. That is what happens to children who dread Monday morning school after the safe relaxation of the weekend: they try not to think about it, and then they wake up on Monday morning with a tummyache. Such a child is not *pretending* to have a tummyache so as not to have to go to school. The tummyache is real. It truly hurts. But, unbeknown to him, it is that same anxious dread in a new form. Unease very easily disguises itself as disease.

New parents who are trying to keep storms of emotion battened down often start out by refusing to acknowledge that anything especially earth-shattering has happened to them. If they can deny that they have any reason to be disturbed or upset, the disturbance itself is easier to ignore; if it is ignored, perhaps it will go away. Such a parent may try to minimize the significance of the birth by saying "After all, nearly everyone has a baby sooner or later. . . ." Of course birth is a natural everyday event if you are taking a worldwide view, but "natural" does not mean "easy" or "insignificant," while the millions of babies who are born every day are not *your* babies. You will only have your first (or second, or third) baby once in your lifetime. For you, having a baby is a unique event.

Trying to play down the emotional significance of the baby's birth and thus sidestep the private feelings it has stirred up usually leads to a frantic desire to "get back to normal." Parents believe that if they can just get through the first extraordinary days and restore old routines, they will feel "like themselves" again.

"Getting back to normal" means different things to different people, of course, and, unfortunately, may mean very different things to a new father and mother. To a man, "getting back to normal" often means getting quickly back to work. Whether he took days or only hours away from his job, waiting to be summoned to take his partner to the hospital, supporting her through her labor, and playing his chosen part afterwards has disrupted his work routine. By going back to it he may be able to distance himself from the extraordinary business of having become a father, swapping the supercharged emotional atmosphere of his home and bed for the reassuringly impersonal sameness of his workplace. He is at home in the evenings and on the weekends, of course, but because of his job he can excuse himself from deep involvement with what goes on there. He is tired after his day's work, after all, so not very much can be expected of him. He has to get up early, so he needs his sleep (ostrich-like, head under the pillow). And when the weekend comes around, there will be plenty of chores to do which are certainly helpful in the practical sense but which also protect him from much feeling or talking about feelings. . . .

Most of the new fathers who behave like this are not uncaring and sexist but caring and overwhelmed.

A new mother has nowhere to escape. She cannot "get back to normal" by reverting to her pre-pregnancy life; that has been over for months, certainly since she became unable to run for a bus or sleep on her stomach. She cannot get back into pregnancy (blissful though parts of that time may have been) because, now she comes to think about it, a lot of that way of life had *birth* rather than *a baby* as its focus. In truth she cannot get *back* to normal in any way at all because the birth has shaken up her life like a kaleidoscope, so that her past lies around her in a thousand gleaming fragments. Her only escape from present chaos is onward: on to a time when she can comfortably share a skin with this woman-who-is-a-mother;

on to a time when mothering her baby feels like normal life. For most new mothers, though, those times are a long way ahead. Months will probably have to pass before those fragments form themselves into a new pattern so that the past, the present, and the future seem to hang together once more.

The kaleidoscope of personal time will form a new pattern for you. You will move on to normal. It will happen faster, though, if you can just let it happen rather than trying to make a new pattern, fragment by fragment, to an old design. Some women cannot bear the timeless confusion of life with a new baby: days which slip by with beds unmade until afternoon, meals scratched together late, and nothing practical accomplished. They talk as if it was a temporary aberration, excusable perhaps by the physical discomforts of stitches which are still sore or breasts which are overfull, but something which they will "get over," like an illness, rather than something which they will "get through" into a different kind of peace. Such a woman may talk as if she was only at home "until I feel better," and pass the early days after her baby's birth planning and replanning an imminent return to her job, a summer hiking holiday, or any project which would require her to be fit, free, and babyless. Ask who is to care for the baby while she is at work, or how she will cope with baby care on a mountainside, and she will look at you with blank anxiety. Her plans are freedom-fantasies, not to be clothed in everyday practicality.

Parents who behave like this are not allowing themselves to behave as they feel, because they are trying *not* to feel so as not to have to cope with *what* they feel.

At the very best, that is a pity because it is a waste of time. You have your baby, but you cannot really begin to enjoy her until you can accept the feelings she has brought with her and begin to approve of yourselves in your new roles as her parents.

This sort of defensiveness may be far worse than a waste of time. Like those schoolchildren whose Monday morning anxiety clothes itself in tummyache, parents who cannot come to terms with their feelings often find them popping up as depression. Postpartum depression is usually described as a female condition starting soon after birth, but baby-based depression is not exclusive to mothers nor to the first days after birth. Both women and men can suffer from it; when they do, their babies suffer, too. Depression closes people off from warm spontaneous contact with others. Babies need this kind of contact with parents almost as much as they need food and physical care. When they do not get it, they are being treated as objects rather than as people. And if they are treated as objects, they cannot make the uniquely personal two-way relationships on which their successful development as human beings, and their parents' ultimate pleasure in parenting, both depend. If parents hold a baby at arm's length and try not to let her change them (because they cannot face their feelings), they will have to try to change her, irrespective of her feelings. If they and their lives are not to adapt to her needs, she must be adapted to fit in with theirs. Hardly surprisingly, the fit is appalling and all three feel the pinch.

Somehow, then, you have to accept your baby the way she is. You have to accept what her existence makes you feel. You have to accept what she needs from you, find pleasure in giving it, and wallow in being a new person's other half. Above all, you have to be open to change, in yourselves and in your lives, because this is probably the biggest change you have made or ever will make.

Unless you are very fortunate in your extended family and the particular community in which you happen to live, you will not get much outside help in making the changeover from couple to family. Society as a whole is confused and confusing about what it wants from mothers and from fathers. Furthermore, while it pays lip service to the importance of children as "the nation's heritage," it seldom seems to concern itself with their well-being or happiness, or to understand the extent of the emotional commitment from parents on which that well-being depends.

Society stresses "individual fulfillment." Women especially are urged to be "aware of themselves," to "fulfill their individual potential," and to beware of the temptation to accept passively what a male-dominated world hands down to them. That is fine, admirable, and necessary. Women do need to be reminded that they are individual human beings with a meaningful personal existence that is not dependent on fathers, husbands, or bosses. Unfortunately, though, women are taught to see individual fulfillment as necessarily embodied in jobs and careers (especially those traditionally occupied by men) and in economic and sexual freedoms which used to be for men only. In the context of competition with men, babies, planted by men and requiring kinds of care associated with old-fashioned housewifery, are an embarrassment. The fact that having and caring for a baby is a vital part of many women's individual fulfillment and creativity is therefore ignored; and where there is *any* social support concerning mothering, you will find it concentrated on helping you out of, rather than into and through, it. You are expected to want to get back to "real work," for example, and if you do want to, you will find people eager to insist on your right to have your job back, three months or six months after the birth. But supposing you *don't* want to go back to your job: supposing you feel that three or six months is not long enough to get a new human being started toward being a person? You will find very few people campaigning for your right to stay with your baby until such time as you feel ready to separate a little. Nobody will replace the income without which your family cannot survive, or accept your right to combine mothering with working and help you to organize the kind of flexi-time or job-sharing which might make that ideal into a reality. If you do stay at home with your baby — whether or not you plan to go back to full-time work when you feel you are both ready — it will be widely assumed that you are staying home for lack of suitable day care. People will campaign to free you to leave your baby, but not to free you to be with her. The banners read "Nurseries for all," not "Nurseries for all who want them and home support for those who do not." No wonder that women who are asked what they do reply shamefacedly: "I'm only a mother." Roll on the day when they can answer confidently, with neither aggression nor defensiveness, "I'm bringing up our baby at the moment."

You will probably find that once you have accepted your new role as mother, talk of "individual fulfillment" leaves you cold, anyway, because you no longer feel yourself principally an individual but your baby's completing half. For a while, at least, the two of you are, and need to be, a unit. You are not in the market for self-fulfillment because "self" and baby are so interlocked that the baby's fulfillment is your own. People who have not had children seldom understand this; people whose children are grown often seem to have forgotten it, while some men, even when they are fathering, never quite know what it is like. Among them all you may find yourself accused of "unhealthy self-sacrifice," "smotherlove," and even betrayal of your sex. It isn't any of those things. When you refuse to leave your breast-fed baby with a bottle and a sitter in order to go out and enjoy yourself, it isn't self-sacrifice but self-protection. While you and your baby are interlocked in this way, you can only be happy if she is happy, so to ask you to leave her, miserable, is to ask you to be miserable yourself. "Smotherlove" prevents a child from emerging as an independent person; it is through being interlocked with you that your baby will gain the confidence to *be* independent of you. "Betraying your sex" means behaving in some way that makes women seem less than men; being someone's mother is not less than male but uniquely, splendidly, female.

Society can be even harder on men-who-are-fathers because the social ideal of equal participation in baby care is contradicted by the social expectation that a man who has a job will be at it all day, five or six days a week. If the mother is caring for the baby all day while he is away at work, the *quantity* of his baby care cannot approach hers. If he is to be her equal as a parent to their baby, his contribution has to rely on its quality, and they both have to make a virtue out of the necessary difference between their roles, accepting that the baby has a mother and a father rather than two identical parent figures.

A man does not have to be with his baby every minute of every day in order to have a close, loving, stimulating, and reliable relationship with her. Indeed, later on, part of the glory of the relationship between father and child may lie in the fact that he is *not* with her every moment and is therefore freshly interesting to her each time he comes home. But in these very early days both parents may resent the difference that his work routine imposes on them.

Because his daily absences are long on the time scale of a brand-new person who is developing from minute to minute, it is difficult for the father to be as aware as his partner of his baby's immediate needs and moods. Since he misses out on so much practice time, it will probably also take him far longer to perfect the practical parenting skills, like supporting that floppy head one-handed, or coping with a really well-used diaper. Those two factors together may well mean that even when he can spend time at home, he finds himself less "good with the baby" than his partner, and may move — or be pushed — into the role of "junior mother" rather than claiming his real place as father.

Do we actually want fathers to be mothers or assistant mothers? That is something you should both be thinking and talking about. The often hidden and unfashionable truth may well be "no."

A lot of women find, often to their own surprise, that however much they want their partners to make a bond with their babies, they do not want to share their own. One put it like this:

I love seeing him with Sara. I shall never forget the look on his face when the midwife handed her to him, even before I'd held her, and I absolutely rely on the fact that he loves her and would care for her, die for her, even if I wasn't around. But that's him doing *his* thing. I

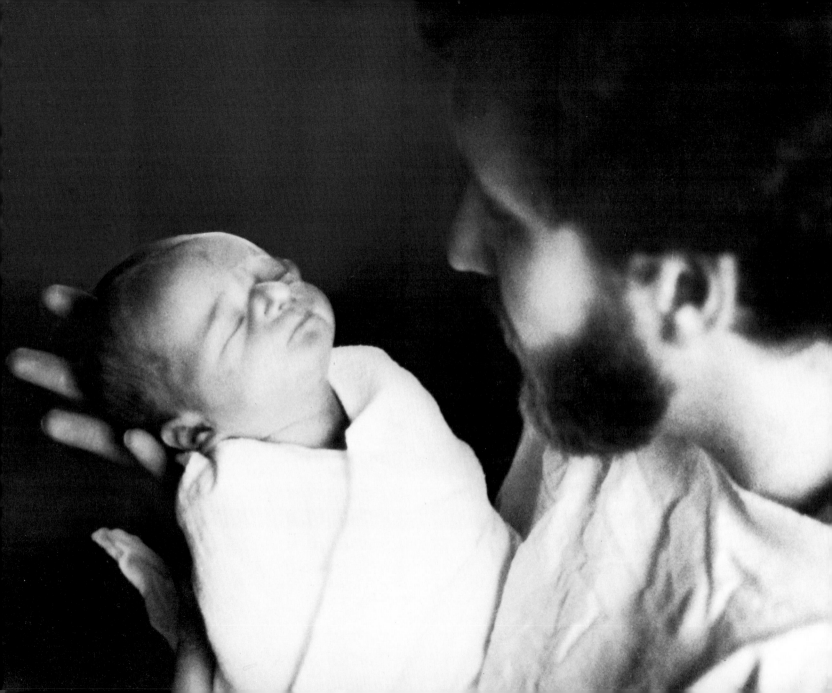

don't want him doing *my* thing *for me*. I don't want him to change her diaper just because he's home and it's his turn and he thinks it will save me the trouble. I just want him to change her diaper when the two of them are together and it needs changing; to do it for *her*, not for me. . . .

Fathers who try to "help with mothering" are often hurt by this sort of reaction. The baby cries in the night, the father gets up to fetch her to his partner, but instead of being grateful she says, "I'll go." Why? Doesn't she trust him to get his own baby up? That mother's reaction has nothing to do with trust; it has to do with the fabric of care and reward-for-care that she and the baby are knitting between them. The mother doesn't want the baby to wake. She probably longs for the time when she will sleep through the night. But as long as the baby needs to be fed, her greeting to the adult who rescues her from hungry discomfort is part of the mother's reward for feeding her. That same mother may find herself slightly put out if, on another occasion, the father gets the baby up from a nap and gives her a drink of water. It is not that the water is *wrong*; perhaps the weather is hot, this is a baby who likes water, and she would have offered water herself. It is that, like a conductor, the mother needs to have the orchestra play to her personal rhythm if she and the baby are to make the best possible music.

A father who has tried to help with mothering and been pushed away by a partner who is weaving her own mothering patterns may find himself edged out toward the practical and impersonal bits of baby care, like laundry, about which the baby knows nothing and cares less. Or he may find himself "allowed" to do almost anything with the baby, but on sufferance and with prior consultation: "Shall I get her up?" "Does she want a bottle?" Neither role will be good for his confidence as a father nor, ultimately, for the relationship between him and his partner.

Many of the fathers who try to share their partners' dawning relationship with new babies, and get their feelings hurt, go on trying because the only alternative they can see is a lonely detachment from the mother-baby pair.

She is your baby but you are not her mother. It is not your heartbeat and smell which may seem comfortingly familiar to her in the first seconds after birth and it is not your breasts which provide her first positive pleasure. Your hormones enabled you to start her off nine months ago, but they are not especially working now for her survival. Watching and listening to your baby and her mother, crooning and purring to each other, small head half-hidden against enlarged breasts, tiny feet scrabbling in the suddenly softened belly which cradles her, you may already sense their bond and feel excluded by it. The baby needs her mother, any fool can see that. The mother needs her baby in a way which perhaps you do not: her body needs the baby and has been preparing for it for months, while your body fulfilled its baby-function long ago. So who needs you?

They both need you, but not as a competitor in your partner's mothering, nor as a competitor with your child who is being mothered. They need you in a unique role which is all yours; a role which society has confused but which remains vital. They need you as partner and as father.

This baby who belongs to both of you needs to wake up to independent life through her mother and to get a firm hold on that life through the mother's feeding, her hormone-ridden vigilance, and her dawning love. As the father, you are the person who can ensure that those needs are met because you are the one who can make it possible for your partner to meet them. She has to risk her individuality and emotions by offering herself to the child. You have to risk your relationship and emotions by openly encouraging her to do so. If you can believe that it is right for the baby that the two of them should be a unit, you will want them to be a unit because you want what is best for your child. And if you can see them as a unit, you will realize that their relationship with each other does not threaten yours with either of them. You are not a parent who is being kept from his child by your partner, nor a lover who is being separated from his partner by your child. You are something far more positive and primitive: a mate standing guard over the den which suddenly contains your family.

People like to believe that "a baby brings a couple together," but it is not always so. The birth of a first child can put tremendous strain on a partnership. Sometimes even those who make it all work out and stick are left with nostalgia for the relationship they shared before the children were born. You can help ensure that your relationship grows with your child, even as she flourishes within it, by facing the unfaceable and discussing the unmentionable.

Face the fact that fathers often do feel emotionally excluded by their partners' involvement with the baby *and* jealous of the attention and mothering that baby receives. Watch out for it in yourself; think about it. You can cope with it if you dare.

You will cope with it better if you realize that mothers are often terrified of the giving over of themselves which a new baby requires. They need to feel that their partners approve, encourage, and facilitate their losing of themselves in the relationship for now. But they also need to know that, because the quicksand of baby love does not engulf men in the same way that it engulfs women, they can trust their partners still to be there, standing on firm ground and ready to remind them of their separate adult selves, when they and their babies are ready for a little more detachment. Watch out for it in your partner and you will know when that time comes.

A woman who, four weeks after a birth, knows that the baby's father is waiting, patiently or impatiently, for her to close the nursery door and turn back into his lover, is torn in two. It may (or may not) be weeks before she really wants to make love, but since it was lovemaking which produced this baby that belongs to both of you, won't loving them both do until she *is* ready?

Parenting is for two grownups.

2 Coming to terms with your newborn

Spare a thought for the baby while you are in labor and especially once you begin to push. Nobody really knows what being born is like, but imagination suggests some pretty terrifying parallels: being a deep sea diver, wedged in rocks during an earthquake, for instance. Whatever image you have of that baby's journey from inside you to the outside world, picturing it will remind you of the *point* of what is going on — which can help you to stay calm and efficient — and will also help you to be ready for the moment when you can do better than *imagine* the baby's feelings because you can *see* them.

Delivery frees you from pain and struggle. It returns to your own voluntary control a body which had been taken over by the birth process. For you it is a moment of relief, but for your baby the worst may still be to come.

Thanks to pioneers like Leboyer and to the readiness of delivery-room staff to rethink traditional practices, the brutalities of smacked bottoms and dangling by the heels have largely been abandoned. Your attendants will be as gentle with the baby as circumstances allow. But however little *they* do, the new environment itself does more than enough.

Lungs which have never been inflated before must fill with air down passages which must rid themselves of amniotic fluid. Nobody knows whether first breaths *hurt*, but it is a very rare baby who can accomplish them without appearing distressed.

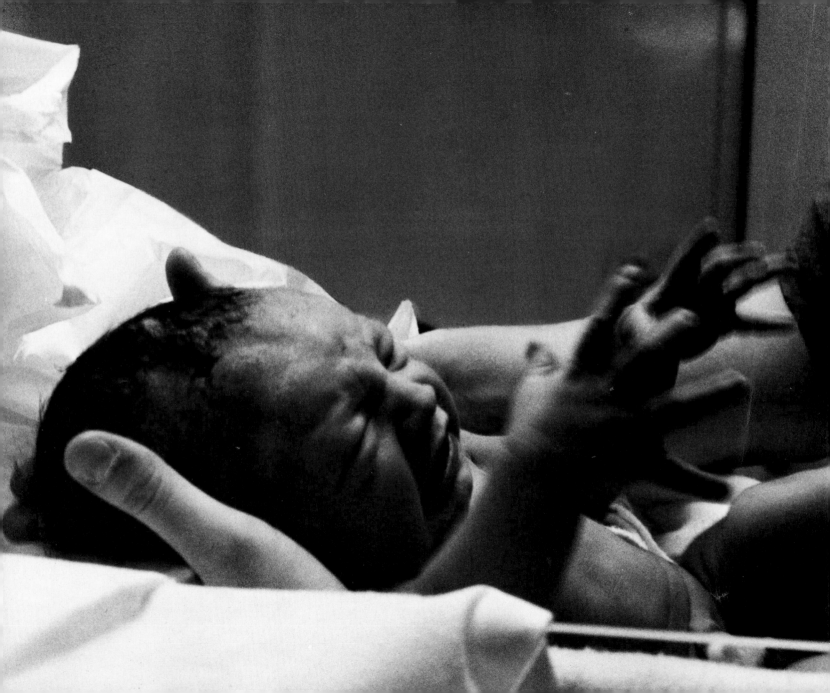

Skin which has always been submerged in blood-temperature liquid will begin to cool as even the warmest air produces evaporation. To prevent too much cooling that skin must be dried and wrapped, and even the softest wrapping must feel like a hair shirt after the continuous soft sameness of your womb.

Eyes, unused in comfortable darkness, are suddenly bombarded with light, and if you watch your baby you will not doubt the pain it causes.

Ears, functional in the womb yet accustomed to sounds muffled by fluid and by your heartbeat and intestinal sounds, are suddenly unprotected from the exclamations, congratulations, snapping of rubber gloves, and clangor of carts . . . your baby jumps and cowers.

Poor baby.

If you are able to feel "poor baby," you yourself can comfort and help your twenty-second-old son or daughter.

Eased out of you and straight onto your belly, the skin which was stretched tautly over him only seconds ago will cradle him; warm and soft against his; smelling familiar, perhaps, and transmitting the constant sound of your heartbeat. Make them prop you up so you can watch him. The new breathing steadies; his heart rate settles; experimentally, perhaps he moves his limbs, discovering for the first time a world in which there is space for him to stretch.

Go on watching and you may see his face relax and those desperately closed eyes open; perhaps he is ready to explore this new environment a little further; perhaps he is not finding it as bad as it seemed.

With a little help you can shift him, gently, very, very gently, into your arms, cradling his head after its bruising journey; supporting the weak muscles of his neck. With your help he can get to the breast and perhaps discover, in these very first minutes of extra-uterine life, his principal pleasure for months to come: sucking.

Not such a poor baby now. A baby who has quickly been shown that there is still comfort in what seemed a world gone mad; that there are even pleasures. . . . The comfort and the pleasure are in you.

The first few minutes outside the womb cannot be like that for every baby. Physical safety must come first and, for their own sakes or their mothers', some babies must be delivered by Cesarean, hauled out with forceps, resuscitated, suctioned, injected. A few who are healthy themselves will be born to mothers who are anesthetized or in some way incapable, just at this moment, of attending to them. If your own physical condition prevents you from greeting and comforting your baby, your partner can claim the privilege for both of you; greet the baby himself and perhaps hold him, close beside your head, so that he is the first thing you see and can touch as you begin to recover. If the baby's physical condition or your own means that the very beginning of his independent life must be spent in expert hands, do not despair; do not even resign yourself to having given your baby anything less than the ideal start because that ideal of "instant bonding" is an extreme swing of the pendulum of birth fashions.

Of course mothers and fathers should be helped to greet their babies the moment they can actually see each other in the world they will share. Of course being the very first to comfort her newborn places a mother exactly where she belongs: at the center of the new baby's existence. But that does not mean that missing those first minutes together will leave a permanent gap in your relationship, a long-term weakness in the bond between you. Women of your grandmother's generation were almost always under anesthetic when they pushed their babies out. Many women today still choose, or accept, unconsciousness. Yet there is no widespread "failure of bonding."

Bonding is not the instantaneous magic bolt parents have often been led to expect. The minute creature with his big, heavy head and soft, curly fingers, his primitive-looking cord-stump and perfect toenails, will certainly turn your heart and stomach over. But what you feel, or what you feel that you are feeling, may be closer to panic or disbelief than to anything you recognize as love. For many, perhaps for most mothers, "bonding" is a learning process; a coming to terms; something that takes time. When there seem to be problems in the bonding between a mother and her baby, they are never due to anything as simple as circumstances or timing. It is feelings which make barriers between people, and it is recognizing feelings and having the courage to look at them which pulls those barriers down.

The newborn baby needs comforting after the physical stress of labor, the physical shock of birth, and those first vital breaths. If none of it went as the mother had planned — perhaps with an induction, lots of monitoring and pain-killing drugs, when her birth plan had been for the most natural possible birth — she may be unable to see her own triumph in producing this living, breathing, beautiful baby through her own sense of failure for not having "done it" as she intended. Preparation for birth can sometimes misfire if the birth comes to seem an end in itself rather than just the means to a baby's safe delivery. If a mother's mind is on her own "performance," on the "fuss" she made, or on what her partner and the staff are thinking of *her*, she may not be able to think about the baby.

The newborn baby needs comforting after the physical stress of labor and the shock of being born. If the labor and delivery have stressed and shocked the mother to a point where she feels in extreme need of sympathy and tender loving care herself, she may have no sympathy to spare for the baby and nothing to give. If sympathy, care, and comfort are not forthcoming for that mother, she may even come to see the baby as the cause of her own distress: an aggressor rather than a victim. With guilt about those feelings added to her physical discomfort, it is hardly surprising if such a mother withdraws from her child and from everyone who tries too soon to persuade her that "the baby's so sweet."

The newborn baby needs comforting after the shock of birth, but if something about his appearance or condition shocks her, the mother may fight off the realization that he is the baby she has been waiting for. An ugly deformity such as a harelip can produce this kind of immediate rejection. The mother needs time, and photographic proof that the lip can be repaired and will look normal, before that rejection can give way to protection.

The newborn baby needs comforting, but if he also needs emergency care, the mother may not dare to feel that she can do anything for him. If he is whisked away to the intensive-care unit, incubated and intubated, dependent for life itself upon machines and the expert staff who run them, she may be quite unable to see any role for herself; unable to feel that this baby is hers.

Feelings like these are normal feelings. They will not remain between a mother and her baby unless, horrified to find that she feels anything but love, she smothers them in silent guilt. Hospital staff can do a great deal to help, but partners who have been involved in the birth can do most of all. Such a mother needs to talk. Often she needs to go over the labor and delivery, blow by blow and more than once, working it through, getting it into proportion, getting used to what happened, and gradually coming to realize that it is over and the baby has just begun. When she can think about him at all (whether that is in two minutes, two hours, or two days), she needs her baby — whatever condition either of them is in. Immediately after an emergency Cesarean she may be in pain, dopey, and attached to drips and drains. She cannot take sole care of the baby but her partner can still place him on her chest and balance him for her while she "holds" him. Unless the baby needs special care, he can then be nursed beside her so that she can watch and listen to every move and sound. Immediately after a traumatic birth, the baby may truly need the warmth and extra oxygen he is getting in his incubator. Perhaps for now the mother cannot hold him, but she can touch him through the glove holes as the nurses do. She can watch him, learn from him, and leave only the technicalities of his care in "expert" hands.

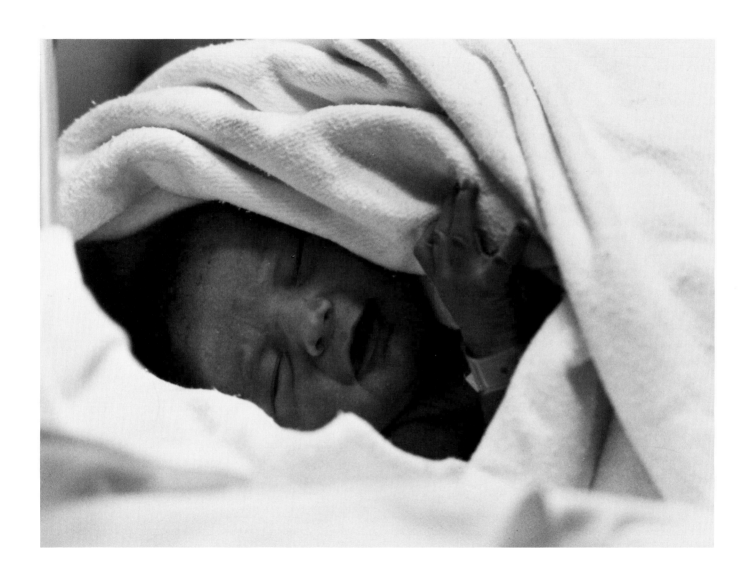

Every mother should be aware that whatever the circumstances she has a basic human right to her baby. She should not have to assert that right because the maternity staff should not need reminding that the two of them need to be together. But sometimes the transfer from delivery room to postnatal ward, or a change of shift among the nursing staff, can lead to unnecessary separation, or just to a mother and her baby being left apart for longer than any physical emergency dictates. Tired, confused, and sore, some mothers would rather put up with anything than ring that bell and "be a bother," while others simply do not realize that if the baby cannot be moved and they cannot yet walk, a wheelchair is an obvious solution. When things have not gone according to plan, the father has a vital role to play just by staying around until he is absolutely certain that his new family is properly settled. If she is desperate for the baby but cannot or dare not ask, who better to do it for her (politely, of course) than he?

Sometimes, on some maternity floors, it does seem as if everybody is determined to keep mothers and babies apart, even when the birth has been "routine" and the baby gives no cause for anxiety.

"Now you have a nice sleep, dear, and we'll look after baby in the nursery."

Why?

If the baby needs something, should the mother not be allowed to find out (or be told) and be helped to provide it?

"She needs her sleep."

Yes, but isn't it for her to decide whether her needs or the baby's take priority? And if the baby needs nothing, but is going to lie there, as many newborns do, wide-eyed and quiet in the enormous world of outside, can he not stay close beside his mother while she sleeps or gazes at him?

"We're just going to keep an eye on her for tonight. . . ."

Does she need watching every moment?

If she does, is the mother not far more likely to be able to keep constant watch than the nurses who have several babies and mothers to care for?

Probably the baby does not need constant watching every minute but is to have regular "observations" of his pulse, breathing, and so forth. Those routine observations can be carried out just as efficiently at the mother's bedside as in the nursery.

One mother had her son delivered by forceps late in the day, insisted on keeping his crib beside her during her compulsory eight hours in bed, and then found herself left alone with him throughout the night. Because nursery care was routine after a forceps delivery, the night staff assumed that the baby was among those who *were* in the nursery and that his mother was peacefully asleep. It was a blessing in disguise:

> He didn't sleep and he was very jumpy; twitchy, almost; not crying but not a bit relaxed or happy. I didn't know what to do for him. I hadn't even been given my "supplies" [of diapers, creams, and so forth]. There was just me and him. I laid him on my chest and put the sheet over both of us and he seemed more peaceful. He put his face into my neck and sort of spread himself out on me and we stayed like that all night.
>
> In the morning the day staff were horrified; said we'd been neglected, and tried to take him to the nursery while they helped me wash and so on. But it was too late. He and I had been together all that night and there was no way they were going to put him in that crib to twitch when he liked being on me.
>
> When I left, I discovered a "remark" on our notes. It said: "All nursing care at the bedside, please. Mother does not wish baby removed." That was a very special night for me and it was obviously a bit special or odd to the staff too. . . .

Many first-time mothers would have rung their bells and insisted on attention during that night because they wouldn't have had enough confidence to let themselves discover that what their babies "wanted" was physical contact with their own bodies. But however terrified you are of failing to notice or to understand what your baby needs, or of missing signs of illness, do try to use the staff and nurses *as a source of information* rather than as expert magicians.

If your brand-new baby keeps crying, you may well want to ask, "Is he all right?" and you may want to ask, "Should I put him to the breast? Is there anything else I can do for him?" Ask, by all means, but listen carefully to the answers before you hand him over to someone else's care. If all your baby would get in the nursery is an "expert's" cuddle, he'll be better off in your arms.

If this is your first baby, try not to let yourself believe that the hospital staff have magic at their disposal which you, a mere mother, cannot command. They have vital training, knowledge, and experience. When all is well they can pass some of it on to you, as and when you need it: the best maternity staff are all teachers, whether they realize it or not. On the rare occasions when all is not well — when a baby is ill or failing to thrive — their expertise, acquired through the care of many babies, will actually be used for your precious one. But in ordinary circumstances they have nothing your baby needs other than reassurance for you. Their skills are a comforting background for your first mothering, but they are not a replacement for it. You will be making the best possible use of that reassurance and comfort if you yourself do almost all the caring while you and the baby are in the hospital. You may be terrified of picking your baby up because of that wobbly head. But permitting a nurse to pick him up and hand him to you will not really help. Pick him up yourself, and you will discover that you *can* cradle his head and gather up the rest of him and that he does not break. You may find it extraordinarily difficult to arrange baby and breast so that one can take the other, but getting a nurse to "put him on," rather than just showing you how, will not help. You offer and, with your help, the baby takes. Breast-feeding cannot use a third party and is often confused by interference. You can do it. You gave birth to this baby; your body is all ready for him. Trust yourself.

You may be entirely confident in your ability to love and care for your baby but a little anxious about your own stamina once you have to cope with home and work and perhaps a (probably jealous) toddler at the same time. If you feel that accepting all the help you can get for the first couple of days will set you up for the next couple of months, trust yourself and get all the rest you can.

Taking your baby home from the hospital can be terrifying. It's amazing how dependent mothers can come to feel on the hospital staff even during a three-day stay. Many secretly dread leaving, and some are even relieved if a minor problem — perhaps a very slight jaundice in the baby — keeps them there for another forty-eight hours. Fathers are not always as helpful as they might be because many of them are not only as frightened of the baby and the responsibility as their partners, but also convinced that those partners must already be practiced mothers after the few hospital days. Shared terror is easier to bear, so there is a lot to be said for letting down your hair and admitting your feelings to each other. Of course the presence at home of somebody you trust, and somebody who has at least *held* a brand-new baby before, is a great help; but if you have your mother or your mother-in-law waiting for the new grandchild, be careful not to go on avoiding the issue by leaving the baby to her experienced ministrations. The ideal postnatal helper looks after *you*, your domestic arrangements, and your visitors, leaving you to concentrate on the baby. She does not rock the carriage while you clean the kitchen floor, nor send your partner out to do the shopping while she helps bathe the baby.

If you can make yourself-and-the-baby your absolute priority, you will soon realize how little it matters if you are thoroughly incompetent for a while. The baby does not care if "nothing gets done" provided he has your attention, your arms, your feeding. The baby does not care if the diapers run out and you have to buy some more in a hurry, or if his day clothes are not washed so that he has to spend the day in his night clothes.

If anxiety does not overwhelm you, competence will come very quickly because, however dependent you felt on the maternity staff, your own home is the place where you are used to coping. The relief of your own bed and bath, coupled with the thrill of seeing that nursery corner occupied, combine to make the whole business of having actually *had a baby* much more real and manageable.

You will not be without expert support. Your obstetrician or midwife will keep an eye on your recovery, while your pediatrician will probably be happy to give advice by phone as well as see your baby when necessary. But, unlike the hospital nurses, they will only advise you in your caring, not offer to do the caring for you. This is your baby. You are his parents. His whole experience of this new way of life is in your hands.

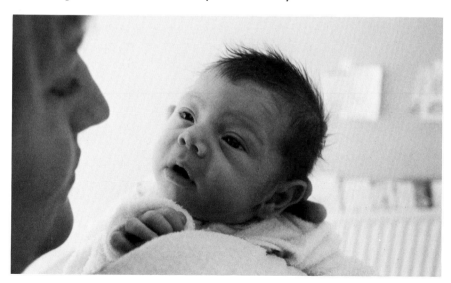

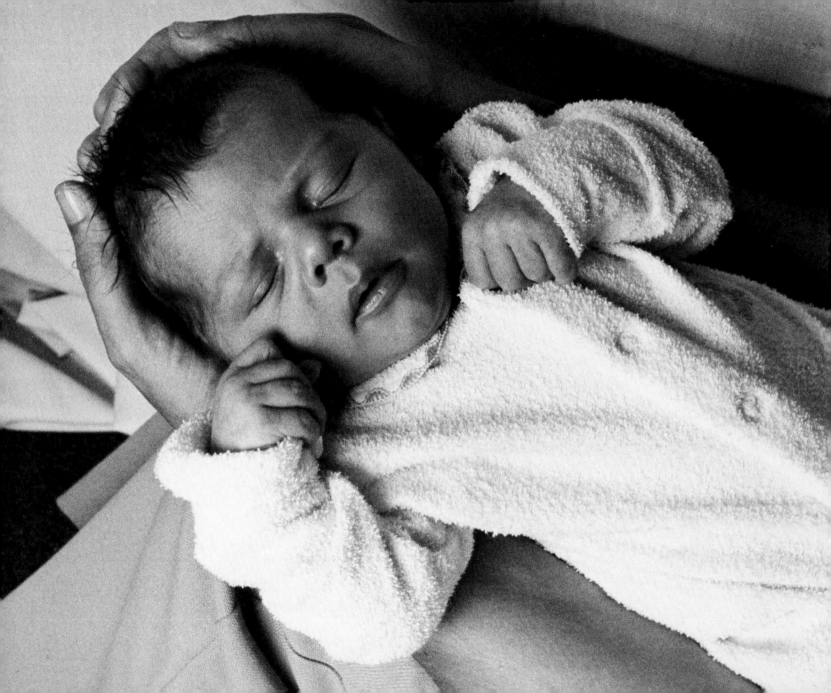

3 Needs and wants

Your new baby is physically helpless.

He is more helpless than a new puppy which can wriggle and crawl to find its mother's milk, or a new calf which can struggle to its feet and follow her. A new human is the most helpless of all baby mammals, and unless you (or somebody) cares for him, he will slowly but certainly die.

Physically helpless though he is, your baby has not come into your world without weapons for his own survival. He cannot take care of himself if you do not; he cannot force you to take care of him if you will not; but he can, almost always, make you want to. His weapons are the feelings he will evoke in you.

Lying there asleep, he is just a baby. A bundle. Sweet.

He may be the fulfillment of a plan or a dream, but he is a baby in the abstract. Yet hold him to you, asleep or awake, his body still almost part of your body which grew him, and he becomes *real;* himself; yours.

The very feel of his body tells yours what to do. Even if you have never held a newborn before, you will hold him gently. Even if nobody has ever told you that his head is too big and heavy for a neck which is still weak, you will find your hand cradling it. Even if you have never consciously thought how cold the outside world must be to a creature accustomed to your internal temperature, you will not strip off those clothes; expose that sensitive skin. Parents can be trusted with their babies.

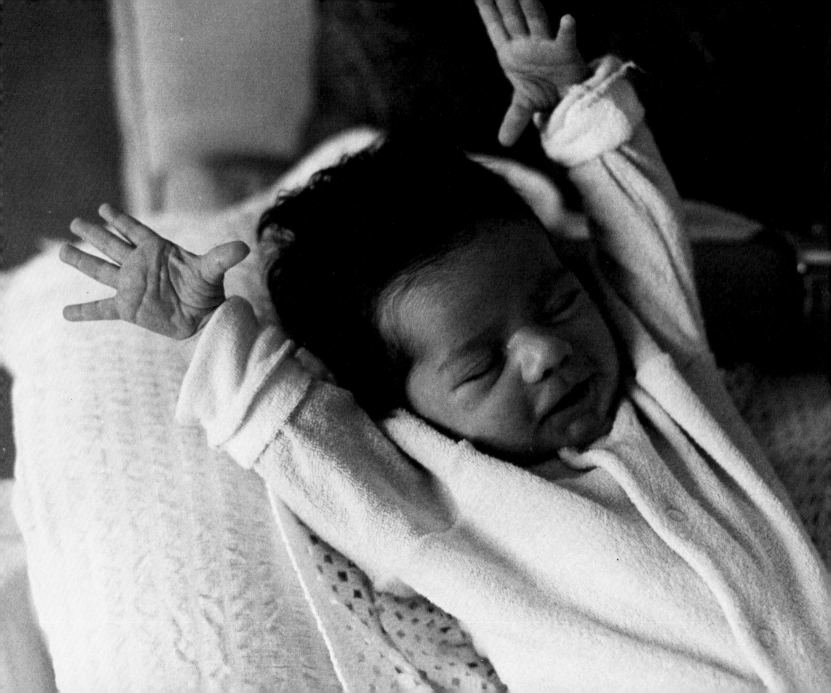

He wakes. . . .

Great dark eyes focus on yours, with a devastating navy blue gaze. Did someone tell you that newborn babies cannot see? Already you know that is nonsense. Your baby is looking, and he is looking at you.

He does not know that you are you, of course. He would gaze in just that way at any adult who was concentrating on him, and it would be a sad lookout for adoptive parents, foster parents, and other loving caretakers, if he would not. What he "knows" is that his very survival depends on entrapping somebody into caring about — and therefore caring for — him. He is "programmed" to look, listen, and respond to you because that ensures that you will look, listen, and respond to him.

These early moments of deep attention do not last for long, but each time your baby lapses back into sleep he leaves you more aware of him as a person. He leaves you holding not just "the baby" but your child.

Your baby is not going to spend his time drifting peacefully in and out of sleep, though. Mystical communication is only a very small part of life with a new baby.

He has needs, and he has to make sure that somebody meets those needs. He does it mostly by crying.

You will not like it when your baby cries, but then you are not supposed to like it.

If you could ignore your baby's crying, you might ignore your crying baby. He needs to be able to get your attention.

If his hunger cries did not affect your womb, breasts, and spirits, you might leave him hungry or thirsty.

If his uncomfortable fussing did not make you forget the comfort of your armchair or bed, you might leave him in the dirty diaper which was beginning to chafe his fragile skin.

If his screams of fear did not shoot adrenaline through your bloodstream, so that you were halfway down the hall before you were even aware of having woken, you might leave him to the real or imagined dangers which, in another place and time, might be snakes or marauding lions.

And if the *prospect of his crying* did not, over the first days of his life, come to haunt the very core of your being, you might never let him teach you how to keep him content. You might even go out and get on with your non-parent life, getting "back to normal" rather than on into a shared way of life.

So he has to cry. He has to cry when he needs you, or something you do for him, so you can be sure that when he does not cry, he needs nothing.

Your baby's crying is your guide, then, not your enemy. It is a signaling system and teaching aid, not noise pollution or a torture technique.

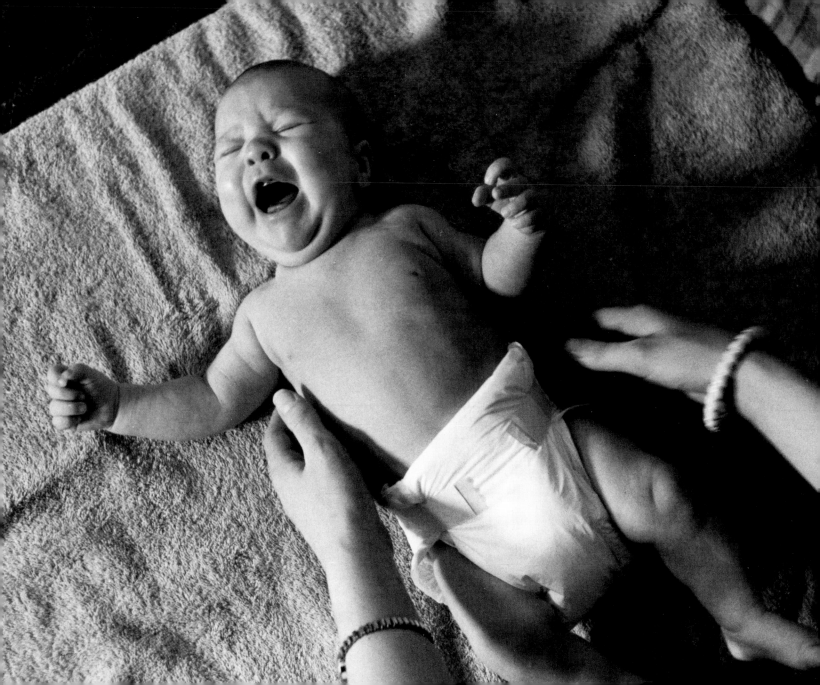

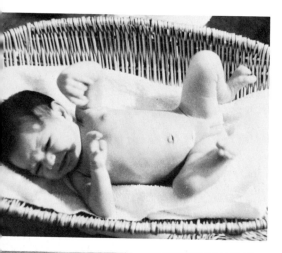

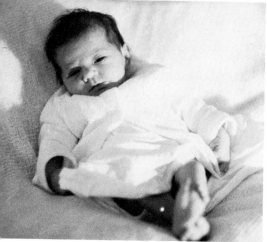

The more you can accept that, the more quickly you will come to understand the signals; to know what she wants when she cries and therefore to be able to give it to her. And that understanding and ability to act will be vital to you as a parent because it will mean that you are confident of your ability *to stop the crying when it has served its purpose.*

Your baby's needs are few and simple. Food and drink in the form of milk to suck. An air temperature which means that, within her clothes and wrappings, her body can hold a steady temperature without having to work to warm or cool itself. Enough hygiene to ensure that she does not gulp bacteria and viruses with her milk and air. Enough cleanliness to keep her baby skin from irritation by her own wastes or city dust. Protection from anything which might hurt or frighten her, and enough cuddling and talking, smiling and singing, rocking and walking, to keep her contented and busy in learning about being human.

Sounds easy, doesn't it?

Sometimes it really is as clear-cut and as easy as that.

Nobody could doubt what this baby was crying about.

She was crying about being exposed without her comforting and protecting clothes, in a hard basket.

It was not difficult to meet the need she was expressing for a bit more softness, warmth, and comfort.

But usually, of course, things are not quite that straightforward. You need to know your baby in order to understand her crying communications, but even when you know her, a lot of guesswork will be involved. Crying alone tells you that she needs something; common sense tells you a lot of possibilities, and knowledge of your own baby turns those into orders of probability. But your baby's crying will not remind you of one kind of loving care nor ask you directly for another. She will just cry until, by a process of elimination, you get it right.

Before long you will even find yourself in disagreement with her over

certain kinds of care which you are quite certain she needs but which she deafeningly assures you are not loving at all but brutal. The two of you may never agree on the need to remove sticky milk from the deep creases under her chin. . . .

She will remind you (often) that food-by-sucking is the most important kind of loving care, and you will probably discover by experience that you can save a lot of time and grief by putting food at the top of your list of answers to crying.

But even here she can be a misleading and inaccurate communicator. You are happy to feed her when (and whenever) she is hungry, but when is that? You will be lucky if she knows herself — let alone makes it clear to you — when she wants to suck but is not thirsty or when she is thirsty but not hungry. . . .

Many aspects of the enormous new world in which she finds herself are surprising, alarming, distressing to her, and when anything upsets her, she cries. Fair enough; her crying is a signal to you that all is not well. But it not only fails to pinpoint the problem for you, it also fails to express its seriousness. Your baby can turn just as stiff and purple over something she momentarily dislikes as over something which really hurts her. She may nearly break your heart over the undershirt which goes over her head as well as over the soap which stings her eyes.

You can buy front-opening undershirts and be more careful with the soap, but you also need enough confidence in yourself as a parent to be able to stay calm when she cries frantically about trivial matters; to say to yourself, "The milk has *got to be* removed from these creases. I'm being as quick and as gentle as I can be, so I'll just get on and get it over." That kind of calm is important. You are not refusing to notice her crying; you make sure you know exactly what her message is. But, knowing what she wants, you cannot, for that moment, give it to her because *you know best about her long-term welfare.* Right now she wants you to stop washing her chin, but if you do, the chances are that later on her chin will be sore. She does not know that, but you do.

Being calm while she cries for something she cannot immediately have will not only help you to do what is right for her — to meet her needs as well as her immediate wants — it will also, over the weeks to come, help her to be calmer about everyday life. Your calmness communicates itself to her. The sponge will not hurt her; the washing will not scar her. Your sureness will help her toward acceptance.

If you can arrive at a basic calmness about your own competence as a parent, it will stand you in good stead at the worst crying times: the times when you cannot immediately understand what it is all about, what she needs or wants.

Those times come to every family because although babies have needs and feelings, and survival instinct tells them to fuss and cry to get those needs met and feelings soothed, they do not know whether the needs they feel are vital to their well-being or not. Your baby has no judgment; no ability to "think" in the way older people think, so she does not fuss a little bit for a small need and at full pitch for a big need. If she is thirsty she will cry. She does not know (nor does her crying reflect) the difference between feeling a little bit thirsty a couple of hours after a good feeding, or feeling dangerously dehydrated after eight hours of vomiting and diarrhea.

She tells you: "Something's wrong. Put it right." But what is wrong and what should be done to put it right *is for your judgment*.

You are the grownups, after all.

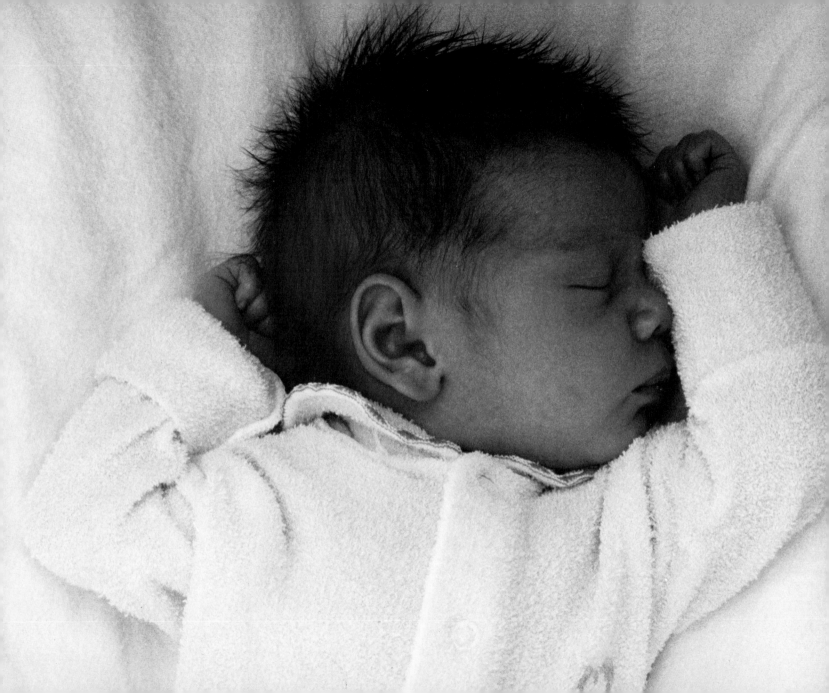

4 Meeting your new baby's needs: complications

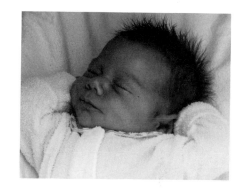

Your baby wakes up.

However blissfully comfortable you made him and however blissfully asleep he was just two minutes ago, what matters now is that he is waking.

Unless he is a very unusual newborn, he is going to need something the very moment he surfaces, and he is going to tell you so, loudly.

He may, of course, have woken just because he has had enough sleep for the moment, in which case he may only need company. But the chances are that he has woken because he is hungry, or at least that the moment he is awake enough to realize anything, he will realize that he is hungry.

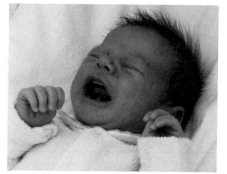

If you go to him and pick him up, talking the idiotic kind of talk one talks to one's baby, the crying will be interrupted. If company was all he wanted (or the change of position that goes with company), the crying will stop altogether and, as long as he stays peaceful, you can assume that you are meeting this moment's need. But if he *is* hungry, he will only quiet for a moment and then the "I'm awake" cry will turn into a roar.

Settle down and feed him, right now, and the total crying time of this whole incident will probably be less than a minute. But if you decide that you must change him before you feed him, the hunger cry will change again, and this time into fury. It is as if he was saying "Is there no way of dealing with this hunger pain? What do I have to do to make her give me my milk?"

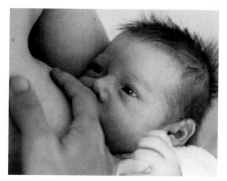

Insisting on changing your hungry baby before you feed him will not traumatize him for life; it will not do him any harm at all in the long run. But it will do *you* harm, right now, in the sense of turning what might have been an entirely peaceful afternoon into a torment.

Furious crying will probably make your hands shake so that you can't get the dirty diaper off neatly and end up having to wash the changing mat. His desperate noise will make you so inefficient that you entangle the sticky tape on the first disposable so that you have to begin again. All this fumbling makes the whole business take longer than usual, too, so your baby will be getting more and more upset.

By this time it must really seem to the baby as if there is no end to his discomfort. As far as he is concerned he has *told* you what he wants, and you have ignored all that and just tormented him instead. He certainly has no margin for error left so that if, in the flurry of it all, you let his head fall back a little or make a muddle of getting his feet into his stretchie, he will probably jump and cry even harder.

At last you put him to the breast or give him his bottle, but it may be too late for him to slip straight into blissful sucking.

His *original* need was for milk to suck, but things may have got more complicated now. All that bawling may have made him swallow a lot of air so that he has to shift it to a more comfortable position or burp it out before he can drink. His nose may be running, too, so that mucus is getting in the way of comfortable breathing once his mouth is full of milk. One way or another you may now have to persuade and help him to take what he needs, and you may even be left wondering whether he really was hungry after all.

When you *know* what your baby wants, why insist on doing something *you* want before he can have it? If he's going to have his feeding anyway, why must he wait? If he is just a little bit unhappy now, why provoke the full-scale unhappiness which will make you both miserable?

If he is really *very* wet, you could always change him when he's had a few sucks to assuage the worst of his hunger. As a routine, the very best time to change diapers is usually between the first and second breasts. The baby gets fed as soon as he is acutely hungry. He gets changed when he is beginning to be too sleepy for sucking, and that wakes him up just the right amount. When the feeding is over he does not have to be disturbed again.

Your baby has been fed and changed, loved, and cuddled. She has been awake a long time so you put her down in her carriage to sleep. Perhaps she sleeps for a few minutes, perhaps she never drops off at all, but she certainly does not settle for a "sensible nap." Instead, she cries.

What does she need?

What is her crying trying to tell you?

What does she want?

You pick her up, and the crying stops.

When she is relaxed against your shoulder, you put her down again and she cries. You pick her up again and the crying stops.

Could the message be clearer? She does not want to be in her carriage; does not want to go to sleep alone. She wants to be held.

Is that too much for a new baby to ask?

It sometimes seems too much for her to ask because Western parents take carriages, cribs, and infant seats for granted and assume that babies will spend a good deal of time in them. It is as well to remember, though, that all these inventions are for adults' convenience rather than for babies' happiness. We have them and use them because we want to be able to put our babies down safely so that our arms and hands are free to do all kinds of things that have nothing to do with caring for them. They may have to accept it, but they don't have to like it.

Throughout most of humanity's history, and in many parts of today's world, babies are *never* "put down" because there is nowhere safe to put them. Mothers hold them, or carry them slung on their backs. When they need to do something else or to have a rest, a relative — adult or child — takes the baby. Western mothers seldom have relations around to share in baby care so they have to use "holding devices" for their babies instead of people. It isn't the same, though. Babies who are always carried get constant living warmth, sound, and movement. They never have to wait for someone to come to them because someone is always in bodily contact. They are never "left to cry" because there is nowhere to leave them and nobody ever tries to delay a response to their crying because the sound, no more than a foot from their ears, makes it impossible for them to hear themselves think. Babies who are cared for in that way cry much, much less than our babies.

With nobody around to share the baby's care and many other things you have to do, you will have to put your baby down sometimes and you will sometimes have to finish changing a toddler's pants before you can go to her, too. But a lot of the time you *could* pick her up and hold or carry her. Even when you are doing chores you *could* take her around with you, slung on your back in a shawl or a Snugli.

A lot of mothers know that their babies want to be held and carried. They know that their own bodies could switch off the torture-sound so that both they and their babies could be happy. They know that they *could* do it, but they don't because they are not sure that they *should*.

You want your baby to be happy. You cannot be happy yourself when he is not, and when he is actually crying, his urgent signals block everything else out for you. So your own feelings and your own self-interest both tell you to do anything and everything you can to answer your baby's messages. When you can let yourself trust those feelings and behave as they suggest, your mothering will fit you and your baby so that between the two of you a personal style, and the weft of your relationship, is woven. But when you cannot let yourself behave as you feel, but try instead to make yourself behave as you "ought," you will be in conflict not only with the baby, but with yourself.

Think carefully about "oughts" and "ought nots" during these first days and weeks of parenting. Think about where they come from and about where they are leading you. If the path does not feel right to you, now that you have a real live baby, you can choose another route.

Think, above all, about the general "ought" which will underpin so many specific ones in the next few months: *"Babies ought not to need so much attention."* Where does it come from?

Perhaps you hadn't expected your baby to take so much looking after. You may have had the impression that new babies sleep for twenty hours out of the twenty-four and wake up only when they are hungry or dirty. The well-broken fourteen hours of sleep which has been your baby's norm so far may have been a considerable shock to you.

But even if you had not expected to be dancing attendance on your baby day and night, that doesn't explain a feeling that all the attention you are giving is *wrong*. What makes you so vulnerable to that feeling?

Trying to hang on to your old way of life

You clearly cannot do all the things you used to do while picking a baby up every twenty minutes, cuddling him for several hours each day, and sleeping yourself for only a couple of hours at a time.

If you have set yourself to live just as you did before the baby came, his cries will interrupt telephone conversations with your friends, work you want to do, the dinner you are cooking, and your favorite TV program. The very frequency with which he wakes and wants attention will interrupt your long-range plans, too, making it clear that you will not be able to leave him with your mother while you take that vacation, let alone ask your neighbor just to keep an eye on him while you go out. . . .

Is it that your baby "ought not" to need so much attention, or is it that you are trying to do too much that cannot be done with him; trying to ration your attention, failing, and then blaming him for the resulting rush, your own exhaustion and the depressing feeling that nothing you do is being done properly?

Trying to fit the new baby into relationships outside the family

Sometimes people outside the immediate family don't realize, or allow for, the practical realities of life with a new baby. If you have always done an elderly neighbor's shopping along with your own, you may find that it does not occur to her that now you have to take the baby along, one household's shopping is quite enough. If you have been secretary of a social or community group, resigning the commitment may be made really difficult for you. Instead of realizing that extra phone calls and letters are the last thing you need, members sometimes say, "But surely you've got plenty of time now that you're home all day?" Even your own families may assume that the pattern of driving to their houses for Sunday dinner will continue — and be hurt when you ask that they save you the trip by coming to your home instead.

If you let yourself feel that these long-established duties must go on despite your newly established baby, or that all those people will stop liking you if you put the baby first, you will run yourself ragged. You have the right to give your baby all the time and energy you feel he needs, and the less outside pressure you have to fight in these first few months, the more likely it is that you will discover space for the outside world very soon.

Trying to build parenting on to partnership

Conflict between your partner and the baby feels all wrong. You know that you and he are the adults of this new family; its joint caretakers. You feel like devoting your whole being to the care of this new person, and even if your partner feels differently for himself (as well as having to behave differently because of the demands of his job or career) you need to know that he *supports and approves of your devotion*, and feels that you do what you do for the baby on his behalf as well as your own. This is why trivial gestures, like bringing you a cup of tea while you breast-feed (*again*), feel so important. He is caring for you *so that you can care for her*, and his wholehearted concern makes the baby equally his, however seldom he can actually be with you both. For the same reason, equally trivial demands ("Where are my clean shirts?") can feel devastating. How dare he demand that you do for him things he could perfectly well do for himself, when you have so much to do for the baby who is helpless? Some fathers do not *know* how much their partners have to do for their babies. Sometimes they do not get the chance to find out, because they are so seldom at home throughout a whole twenty-four-hour period. Before (or after) you have flown into a rage over those shirts, do tell him, show him, give him the chance to see. If you are amazed at the amount of attention your baby needs, why shouldn't he be? If every father could have at least a couple of weeks' paternity leave, this kind of problem would be much rarer.

Conflicting emotional demands can be even more painful than conflicting practical ones. If your partner makes you feel that he would sometimes like the baby out of the way for a bit so that you can really *listen* to the latest office scandal or union campaign, you will feel that he is subtly criticizing the baby for being overdemanding. However critical you may sometimes feel of your baby's behavior, the slightest hint of criticism from anyone else will raise your hackles and shake your confidence in your own mothering, so that hurts.

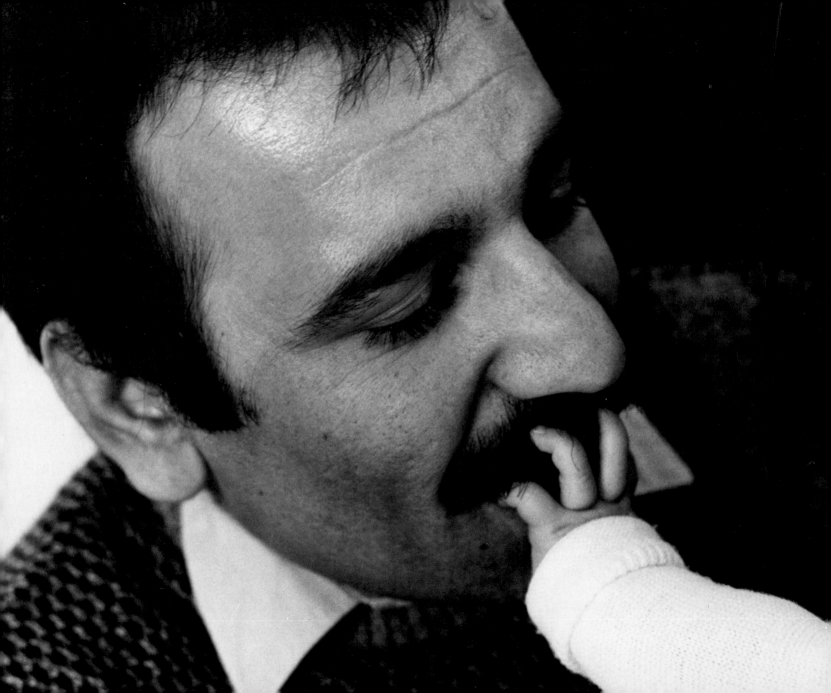

But feeling that your partner sometimes wants the baby out of the way (and your thoughts) so that he can have back the separate, adult you is not as painful as feeling that he wants the baby out of the way so that he can have her place. The worst kind of conflict between a new baby and a partner is certainly the kind where you feel you are being asked to *mother them both*. Parenthood is for adults but none of us is ever grown up all the way through. There is always a layer of personality which remains needy, dependent, and egocentric. Deep down, we all need our mommies and daddies. It is easier for most women to function on a grown-up level with their new babies than it is for most men. After all, your body is involved in this supremely adult function; your hormones are maintaining your readiness to mother; your adult sexuality has reached a culmination which is entirely appropriate. It may be different for your partner. It may even be that that adult sexuality of yours, those milk-filled breasts, for instance, do not make him conscious of his adult role as your sexual mate and the father of your joint family, but instead throw him straight back to long-buried memories of his own mother and his own infancy. Many men lack a model of fathering because their own fathers were little involved. Faced with a mothering woman and their own baby, some flounder.

Answers cannot lie in desperately trying to give your partner what he needs if what he needs is inappropriate to his role as father. To play at "you're my big baby" is only to confuse the issue, make yourself secretly angry with him, and eventually prevent you from doing what you feel is right with the baby. Answers have to come from helping troubled partners to look at their own feelings and to move deeper into fathering. You are partners. In most partnership conflicts, decisions should be equally balanced. But not here. Here the baby tips the balance. You *must* mother that baby as openly and fully as you want to mother her, and the more your partner can father her, the more likely it is that mere tolerance will give way to real involvement and jealousy will drain away.

Trying to cope when there's also a toddler

Although a few of them conceal it, *all* toddlers are jealous of new babies. Don't waste precious energy on feeling guilty and regretful when yours shows resentment, and don't risk making matters worse by trying to persuade him to pretend that he loves the baby as you do. Up to now he has been your baby, and you have been his mommy and daddy. He has never, in all his short life, wanted another mommy or daddy, so how can he understand that you could want another baby? You are enough for him; how can he fail to feel hurt when it becomes clear that he was not enough for you? "We love you so much that we want another baby just like you" won't wash, any more than it would placate you if your partner said, "I love you so much I can't wait to have another husband/wife like you."

"You're my big grown-up boy now" will not help either, any more than "You're my experienced old partner now" would help you. If you try to make him join with you in parenting the newcomer, you only make matters worse because, just at the moment, he feels that his "grownupness" is his whole trouble. If he were tiny and helpless, like the new baby, maybe you'd devote yourself to him as you do to her.

Pretending that you *don't* love the new baby as much as you do is a mistake too, even though it may sometimes feel like being tactful. Your toddler must see you as a good and loving mother; a fulfiller of needs; a responder to messages. To show him favor, by ignoring the baby's crying while you finish a game or a cuddle, for example, may placate him for that moment but will actually frighten him for the future. If you are not reliable for the baby, can he be sure that he himself can rely on you, or are there perhaps some circumstances under which you would ignore *his* distress?

Your toddler must come to understand that love and care are not rationed. He must learn that people can love more than one other person. It is only by this route that he can eventually come to see that your love for the new baby does not threaten or impinge on your love for him. Yes, there will be practical, superficial time constraints; times when she needs picking up in the middle of his story, or when her hunger curtails his bath or delays his walk. And there will be times when her sheer presence on your lap blocks his way to a proper cuddle. But it is out of his awareness that you *always* do your best to meet *both* their needs — tucking the baby under your arm while you help him, fetching her to feed while you read to him — that his security will return. If you also help him to see that the special things the baby gets (the breast or a bottle; diapers, talc, a tiny bath, and crib) are things that meet her needs but not his, just as his special things (stories, wheeled toys, rough-and-tumble games, food on a plate) meet his needs but not hers, he will soon come to feel that he has nothing to be jealous about. The baby is welcome to look at his toys, but they are too heavy/complicated for her so she does not routinely use them. He is welcome to a taste of her special milk, a sit in her bath, or a sprinkle of her talc, but his own things are actually more fun for him.

Your toddler, whom you love and whose jealous pain hurts you, will not therefore be helped by your trying to quash and conceal your feelings for the new baby. And trying to quash or conceal those feelings may actually hinder you in coming to terms with your new family. Most mothers regret their inability to devote a hundred percent attention to their second babies. A great many actually wonder whether they will ever love No. 2 with quite the searing intensity with which they love No. 1. Trying to be "tactful" about surges of emotion, moments of pure amazement at the beauty of your new creation, or sudden overwhelming urges to plant kisses on starfish paws, may actually delay the time when the second child's hold on your heart is secure.

Loving a two-year-old more than a two-day-old is natural, almost inevitable. You have had two years to get to know the toddler and no time at all to get to know the baby. But the *potential* for loving that second child is there; it may even be stronger this time than it was when the whole business of motherhood was new to you. The truth of your situation is that

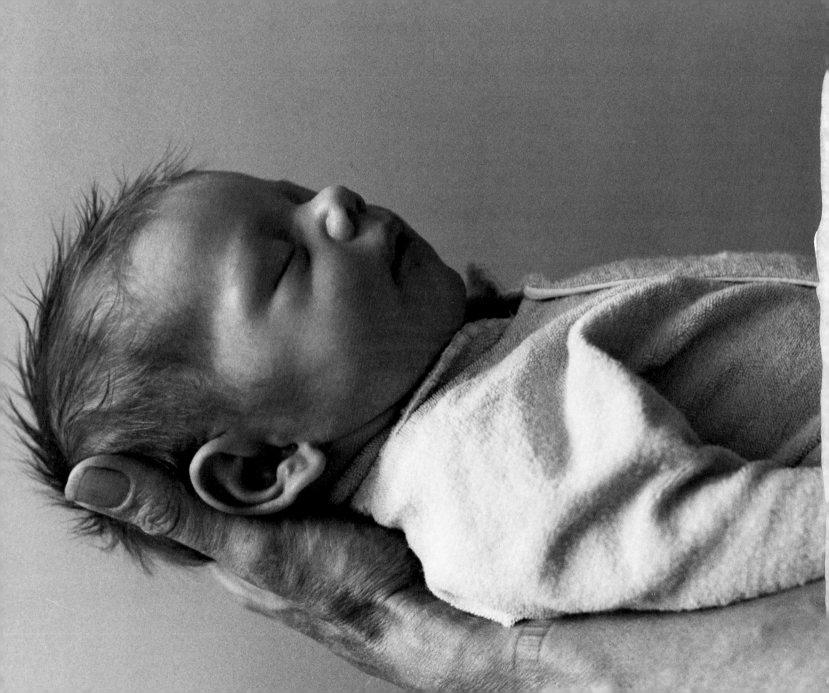

you are a family and there is love enough for everybody. You will all be happier if you can let that show.

The question of spoiling

Maybe your conflict over giving your baby everything she seems to need/want comes out of a feeling that indulgence is bad for *her*. Although some of the parents who talk of their determination not to "spoil" their infants are really trying to protect themselves from being "put upon," others long to indulge their babies yet are haunted by the specter of spoiling.

If well-meaning relations and advisers tell you not to pick her up all the time because "you'll only make trouble for yourself later on"; not to take any notice when she cries because "babies are canny"; and not to keep getting up in the night because "she's not the only pebble on the beach and you need your sleep," don't just take their words at face value. Think about *your* baby; think about *yourselves;* and think about what "spoiling" actually means.

It is not possible to spoil a *baby.*

Spoiling is about the power relationship between a child and her parents. A spoiled child sets herself to get what she wants against the wishes or better judgment of her parents. She says to herself, so to speak, "If I make enough fuss, I can *make* her buy me some candy"; "If I go on and on and *on* at him, he'll give in"; "If I keep pulling his newspaper away, he'll give up and come and play with me"; "If I whine and pull at her and keep interrupting, she'll stop talking to her friend and pay attention to *me.*"

In order to set herself to get what she wants, when it is the opposite of what her parents want, the child has to be old enough and mature enough *to know what her parents want*. She has to have reached the stage of development when she is able to put herself in somebody else's shoes.

A baby cannot do this. Even when a baby knows what *she* wants, she does not have any idea what *you* want; what your feelings are.

Therefore a baby cannot be spoiled.

If you give a baby everything she appears to want, you are teaching her confidence that the world is a good place where her needs will be met.

All the evidence we have (and there has been lots of research done, all over the world, on how often babies cry under what circumstances) points in the same direction: babies who are always attended to quickly and pleasantly demand less attention and cuddling, not more. Truly.

Sometimes when you are thinking about this, it helps to look at your behavior toward your baby in terms of the "messages" it gives her in answer to the "messages" you get from her crying.

Suppose that you have fed, changed, and cuddled her, and put her down, half asleep, in her crib.

A few minutes later (probably just as you serve a meal), she begins to cry. You go and pick her up. She stops crying, burps, and relaxes. You put her down again.

Five minutes later the same thing happens.

If you go to her again immediately and pick her up just as you did before, what is your message?

I don't quite know what it is you want or why you aren't settling down to sleep, but if you cry I will always come and do anything I can to make you comfortable and happy.

If you do not go, or delay going for several minutes, what is your message?

I don't know what you want, and I am not interested in finding out. I know there is nothing the matter with you [because your physical needs have been met], so however much you cry I shall ignore you.

From the baby's point of view, as far as we can work it out, how must those messages appear?

I'm uncomfortable/unhappy/bored. I make my unhappy (crying) noise and the one who makes things better comes.

or:

I'm uncomfortable/unhappy/bored. I make my unhappy (crying) noise but nothing happens. I go on making it but nobody comes. Nothing happens to make things better. I am helpless.

When you go at once to your baby and give her what she needs, she stops crying because she has nothing more to cry about. She will not cry again until she needs something again. And she will not cry every time she is left on her own because she will have no reason to fear being left alone and helpless.

If you do not go to your baby she will not *decide* to stop crying. The chances are that she will not stop crying at all so that eventually, after three or five or fifteen minutes' crying, you go to her after all. But if she should stop before you get there, it will not be because she has learned a valuable lesson but because she became exhausted. Being left to cry herself to sleep is not likely to persuade her that her crib is a pleasant place to be; over a few weeks she may begin to fuss the moment you try to leave her.

So if you always go to your baby, you are not *spoiling* her. You are showing her that the world is a good, safe, caring place that she shares with good, reliable, caring parents *with whom she can always communicate.*

If you refuse to go to her, you are not teaching her not to cry, you are teaching her to cry more and more and feel herself helpless, because, however many messages she sends, *she cannot communicate with you.*

5 Wallowing in early smiles

However much attention your baby is asking for, she is not asking for more than she "ought." If it is more than you can give her while you live as you lived before she was born, it may be your way of life which needs altering, not your baby. If it is more attention than people outside your family can spare you to give, their expectations must change, not the baby's. If it is more attention than your partner wants you to spare from him, then he must find a way to spare more for both of you so that he comes to understand that you are both parents now as well as partners. Paying attention to your baby will not spoil her. Wallowing in being her mother will not spoil you. The two of you are supposed to be interlinked, with the lines of communication between you permanently open. There is no "busy signal" or "no reply" between you. You don't have to hold back from her in case she submerges your individual adult self altogether, or hold her away from you in case she never becomes independent of you. Your individuality will re-emerge of its own accord once it has had enough of reveling in being half of somebody else, while her independence as an individual can only develop if somebody lends her a part of themselves to depend on.

There will be people who will tell you that "you're getting very boring now that you only think about babies"; you may even be asked whether you are on your way back to work as you leave the house for your postnatal checkup. Ignore them. You are caught in a magic circle which no

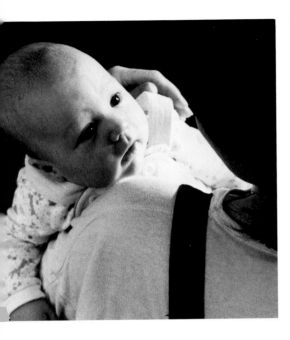

outsider can understand and which makes most outsiders at least a little jealous. If they think it is boring, or degrading, or a waste of time to have life temporarily dominated by something the size of a bag of potatoes, laugh and let them. They don't realize that your baby is a person.

She is, though, and just about now you are going to get to know that person in a new way. You already knew that she was yours, that she was your own special miracle of creation and that she could summon you with a whimper and plunge you into despair with a sad cry. But did you know that you were hers, that you were her special people and that she could overwhelm you with joy with a smile? If you didn't know all that it is probably because your baby hasn't begun to smile yet. Until she does, the language of her pleasure and of her developing love is not as invasive as her crying. You notice when she is unhappy, notice when she is contented, but scarcely know the other side of the coin: her positive happiness.

Watch her when she cries and you go to greet her. She stops crying when she hears your voice, but now, when you pick her up, she doesn't just study your face with a solemn newborn stare, she watches you, looking into your eyes, watching your lips move as you ask her the idiot-questions of all parents everywhere: "Who's a beauty baby?" Her face softens, brightens, you can see that she is pleased. Hunger may cut your "conversation" short, but when the worst of it is satisfied, she makes it clear that it is not just your delicious milk that pleases her. Burping her or changing her diaper at halftime takes longer and longer because she wants you to put your face where she can see it; she wants to "talk" to you.

One day her bright, interested face suddenly lights like the first flickering flame of a new fire. She smiles and in that one magic moment you feel warmed, and rewarded in full measure, for all the work and worry, stress and exhaustion of her first weeks. *She is smiling at you* and it is almost like greeting her all over again as you did when she first emerged out of your body. She has emerged from the strangeness of being a newborn and, with a single smile, she has joined you as a real human being. If you haven't quite got there yet, you may think it absurd to make such a fuss about a mere smile; but when you get there and it happens, you will love that smiling face more than you have ever loved anything before and you will remember it as one of the vital punctuation marks of parenthood.

Suddenly there is a new point to everything you do for her: her pleasure as well as her well-being; your pleasure as well as your responsibility. And suddenly you can believe that, from her point of view, you are a "good mother" or a "good father." Confidence floods in.

The more your baby offers you smiles which make you feel like that, the harder you will work to please her. The more you please her, the more smiley (and the less fussy) she will be. And, of course, the less fussy she is, the more you will *want* to please her. Between you a pleasure-circle will be woven, bit by bit, until you have quite forgotten the feeling that she was a strange and alarming creature who might blow up in your face if you made a mistake, or break if you dropped her. You come to feel that you and she can cope with each other and that, as long as you are together, all will be well. That feeling of being able to cope is the beginning of your real parenting. When it comes, you will know that you have dragged yourself out of the swirling chaos of having a brand-new baby.

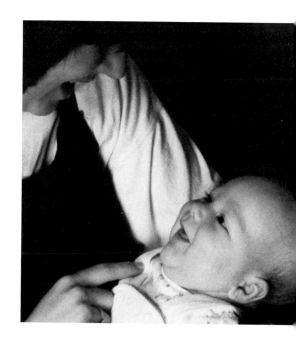

New babies create chaos because they are chaotic themselves. They have no baselines, no established patterns of behavior. They are adapting to the outside world, recovering from birth, moving into independent life; and, while they do so, Monday's behavior bears no relation to Tuesday's, and a long sleep this afternoon does not predict more sleep or less sleep this evening. Only as babies settle down and begin to pattern their behaviors, their sleeping and waking, their feeding and crying, their looking and listening, can parents begin to feel that they know them and understand them. Only when you can feel that you know your baby can you really begin to love her (who loves a stranger?), and only when she smiles as if to say that she loves you too, can the whole relationship really take off.

Once that moment comes, once you know what to expect of your baby (even if it is the worst!) and know how to cope with her (even if it takes you all you've got), your baby can be easy, for you and for herself, even if she is very far from being "easy" or a "good baby" in the conventional sense.

A baby can be "born easy," of course. That usually means that she adapted easily to the outside world and did not seem to find it terrifying or overwhelming; that she had no problems with her digestion and that, all in all, she found it satisfactory to eat and sleep, grow and flourish. Parents with a baby like that (and there are *a few*) are obviously likely to start building their confidence and reaping rewards more quickly than parents with jumpy or colicky or generally miserable babies. But although it may take longer, you can build that confidence and reap those rewards *whatever your baby is like*, if you can be proud of yourself for handling her as she needs to be handled, enjoy the joy you give her and she gives you, and refuse to take any notice of anyone who tells you to "do it by the book" instead of by the baby.

Perhaps your baby does not sleep very much. Perhaps she never sleeps for more than four hours at a time in the night or more than an hour or so at a stretch by day. That can be confusing, maddening, soul-destroying in the very first weeks when you don't *know* how long she will sleep nor what to do with her when she wakes. But now that you know this is her pattern, and now that you can always keep her happy, playing in her carriage, sitting on your hip, or slung on your back, who cares?

Your baby may eat rather often. Far from having a feeding every four hours, and skipping at least one in the night, she may want to eat ten or twelve times in the twenty-four hours. If she sucks enthusiastically and makes you feel good for having such perfect stuff to give her whenever she wants it, what's the problem?

Maybe your baby is very alert, so that she is easily distracted from sucking by visitors, easily woken by passing planes, and incapable of sleeping when she is out in her carriage. At the very beginning, when you can only relax while she sleeps, a baby like that can make you try to tone everything down so as to disturb her as little as possible. But now that you know you can always cope with her, it is different. If she wakes, you can either soothe her back to sleep or get her up to be companionable. If her feeding is interrupted, you can always give her a bit more when she's ready. If she doesn't sleep while she's out she will sleep later if she needs to. . . . Knowing that you can cope with her means that you don't have to worry and fuss, and if you can stop yourself from worrying and fussing, you can have fun even with the most "difficult" of babies.

It is not only babies' behavior, new parents' confusion, and the stresses of adapting to the new role of "parent" which can prevent you from reveling in your baby. Outside pressures can also get in your way. Everyone has been a baby; most adults have had babies. Most of them therefore think that they know how babies "ought" to behave and "ought" to be brought up. A lot of them will tell you, whether you ask them or not.

They will tell you that your baby *ought* to be sleeping through the night; that she *ought* to have given up any (let alone three) night feedings; that she *ought not* to suck more often than every four hours in the day. If your confidence as a mother is still only skin-deep, such people may puncture it. You probably go on doing exactly what you were doing before because it is not only you who decides when your baby should suck, and your "advisers" did not tell the baby what to do, they only told you. But instead of doing it happily and being rewarded by your baby's happiness, you may do it reluctantly and spoil things for both of you. They may even turn your pleasure-circles into vicious-circles. Let's look at how easily, how subtly that can happen.

It is 1 a.m. Your baby wakes and cries.
She is asking for a feeding.

If you are allowing yourself, and being allowed, to do what feels obvious and right, you get up and go to her, right now. She stops crying as you pick her up and settle her at the breast. She sucks and you feel the milk pouring down in response to her. When her first urgent hunger is stilled, she opens her eyes and searches your face; perhaps she even releases the nipple while she grins at you, stretching like a comfortable kitten, knowing there is more when she is ready. You change her diaper, put her back on the second breast, watch her suck herself to sleep. . . . Half an hour after that first summons you are back in bed yourself.

If you are trying not to answer her call, trying to persuade her that she "ought not" to have what she is asking for, you don't get up right away, but bury your head under the pillow, trying not to hear, trying to quiet your ready breasts' response to her summons. Perhaps you stay there for as much as ten minutes; perhaps it is only five minutes but feels like forever. Either way it's enough. You do not stay there and let her cry it out even if your partner is not muttering and your neighbors are not banging on the wall. You do not because you cannot. Eventually, then, you get up, but you are guilty and fed up. Guilty at having left her to cry, and guilty for not having left her longer. Fed up because you have fought a painful battle and won nothing.

You are greeted by hiccuping sobs. Instead of putting her straight to the breast, you must first try to calm her enough to suck. Eventually she will latch on, but her breath keeps catching and her nose is running so she cannot suck with her usual smooth power. Tired with all that crying, she cannot stay awake for long before her need for food is overtaken by her need for sleep. After all that misery she has not had a full feeding. You have been awake much more than half an hour and you will probably have it all to do again in an hour or two.

You are the only person who knows, has, and gives what your baby needs. You can collect other people's opinions and advice, even use them when they happen to fit with *your* feelings, and *your* baby; but you will be better off ignoring anyone who tells you what you and your baby ought to do. There are no "oughts." There is only what works for both of you.

Be warned: you may find it far easier to ignore the "experts" on TV and in the baby books than you find it to ignore your own mother, your partner's elder sister, or your own old friends. You want everyone who matters to you to think that your baby is absolutely perfect and that you are a perfect mother. Grandmothers who refuse to dote and who implicitly criticize the baby and your mothering with cries of "You're running yourself into the ground, dear," can be very, very hard to cope with. It is as if they refused, even now, to acknowledge you as a full adult, but still felt that they had a right to tell you what to do "for your own good." You don't want to be treated as a child anymore, but you do want adult support and love to balance the support and love you are pouring into your baby. If people who love you really think you are getting too tired or too stressed, you want them to help by taking some other responsibility off you so that you have more time for the baby. Suggesting that you give the baby less is the opposite of helpful.

At this unique stage of your life, everyone who truly loves you must love your baby, and as the weeks pass, you will probably find that you have re-sorted your close friends on that basis. Perhaps you can put up with the people who come and talk to you about their own affairs over your nursing baby's downy head, or who hold you at the dinner table with boring stories after that summoning cry has sounded. But the people you will really want to see are the ones who want to watch and touch and share; the friends who love your baby because she is part of you, and who want to know her because they love you.

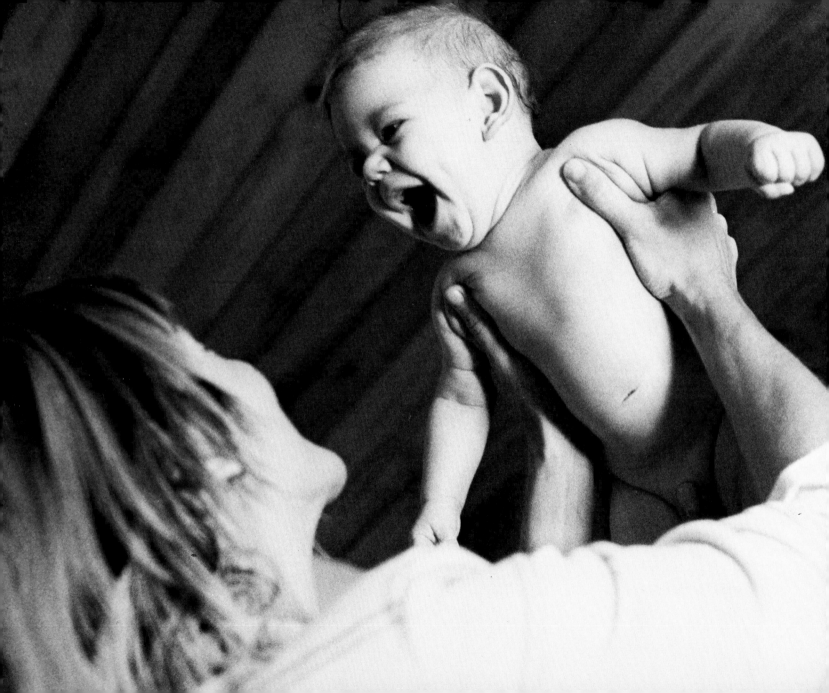

6 Tuning in to your baby as a person

Allowing yourself to wallow in the feelings your new baby arouses in you, to revel in the miracle of his existence and in your own ability to understand what he needs and give it to him, will certainly get you all off to the best possible start. But it would be foolish to pretend that such a start will automatically make you the contented parents of a happy, flourishing child. Babies vary. Parents vary. The people who make up families cannot choose each other, so the ease with which they fit together varies, too. If you are a sociable, outgoing, physically active person, you will probably find it far easier to tune in to a placid, confident baby than to a rather jumpy and retiring one. But if you are rather quiet yourself, you may be ideal for that jumpy baby and inclined to let the placid one get bored. Whether you and your baby are temperamentally similar or very different, you will end up by meeting in the middle because you will learn from each other, and eventually evolve a "style" that is comfortable for both of you. But tuning in to your baby, so that you can teach him and learn from him, takes interest and thought, brain as well as heart. It can be difficult.

When a math student finds a problem too difficult to understand and to solve, she is tempted to turn to the back of the book and write down the printed solution. She has an answer for today but she has done nothing for her skill as a mathematician. When you find your baby too difficult to understand, and problems in caring for him both urgent and insoluble, you too may be tempted to go looking for easy answers, but you too will find that just accepting them does nothing to build your relationship with your child. When you go outside yourself and your own feelings in search of help with your baby, you have to realize that however expert or experienced your adviser may be with babies-in-general, only you have expertise or experience with your particular baby. People may be able to give you useful information to add to your thinking, but nobody can do that thinking for you. They may be able to suggest useful alternative courses of action, but they cannot tell you which to choose. They may be able to tell you what most babies like or dislike, do or don't do, but they cannot tell you how your baby feels or what *he* should do. Making the best possible use of outside help absolutely depends on staying tuned in to your baby and interpreting outside advice for him, and him alone.

Is my baby ill?

Sick babies need medical help and they need it quickly. Any parent who thinks there may be something physically wrong with a baby is always right to go to the doctor's office, or to the nearest telephone.

There is absolutely no shame in making unnecessary calls because small babies' symptoms are often quite different from those of older children. An infection that would give a schoolchild a high fever and make him restless and irritable may cause a baby's temperature to drop dangerously low and make her very quiet and lethargic. So, deciding whether a small baby is ill is not a matter of listing symptoms or looking them up in a book which does not specify age groups. It's a matter of deciding whether the baby's behavior seems different from usual (even if you haven't had her around long enough for anything to be very usual), or whether there is something about her which makes you feel uneasy, even if you cannot quite pin it down. Your unease is a good enough reason to ask a doctor or clinic to see her.

If the doctor finds something physically wrong with your baby — a middle-ear infection, for example — you are using his expertise in two ways. You need that expertise to make the diagnosis, because you cannot inspect your baby's eardrum and she could not even tell you what hurt her, she could only "say" (deafeningly) that something did. And you need that expertise to prescribe treatment for the infection. But even when the doctor has told you the diagnosis and the treatment, he has not taken over *your baby's care*. She must have the medicine he has prescribed, but you will have to persuade her to take it. He has told you that she is in pain, but you will have to help her bear it. He has told you, perhaps, that the infection must be treated in a hospital, but you must go too because you cannot dispatch the ear without the baby and the baby needs *you*.

A lot of small babies are brought to doctors because they are very discontented, because they cry a great deal without obvious reason, or because they have periodic screaming fits during which they look as if they are suffering from acute abdominal pain.

Many of these babies are not sick. They cannot be given any direct medical help. Doctors look them over and tell parents that there is nothing wrong.

For some parents, that assurance is enough. They have used the doctor's expertise in diagnosis to make quite sure that they were not missing anything. Now they can return to their own expertise to help the baby get through a bad day or a bad patch: to help her to feel happier. But for other parents, especially those whose confidence in themselves has already been eroded, an assurance that their baby is not physically ill is not enough. It may even make them furiously angry.

How can he *say* that there's nothing the matter with her when she keeps on screaming like that?

She wouldn't say "he's fine" if she had to sit up with him half the night.

Parents who feel like that are tuning out and looking for an easy answer. They want a label; a name which will describe their baby's behavior to them; a diagnosis which will not only explain the crying or unhappiness, but also make it clear that it is not their fault. If the doctor diagnoses "colic," for example, they will go home feeling far more contented even though the baby is as miserable as ever.

In all the arguments you may hear about what colic is and even about whether it exists as something separate from a variety of other early discomforts, try to remember that it is your baby's distress that matters, not the name by which you call it. A screaming baby needs your sympathetic concern and your creative attempts to make her more comfortable. She needs all that whether she is suffering from unusual sensitivity to the essentially normal contractions of her own gut or to any other internal discomfort.

If you can be *more* sympathetic and creative because you call her "colicky," fine. A little later on you may find it easier to tolerate endless night waking if you say she is "teething," and easier to stay cheerful through daytime crankiness if you put it down to upset from her immunization shot.

But medical-sounding labels do not always make creative sympathy flow more easily. They sometimes make parents feel that all the baby needs is a quick rub of the gums with teething gel or a dose of paracetamol syrup. While being given "medicine" can be part of a baby's experience of loving care, it cannot stand in for it. So, if the medical label means that you use a dose of this or that *instead* of efforts to pour comfort into her from yourself, that label is not helping you to help her. It is letting you off the hook by giving you a solution from outside you both rather than a solution from inside your relationship.

Outside explanations and "solutions" will always create more problems than they solve if you listen to them instead of listening to your baby. The less you listen to her, the less you will understand her. If she seems to demand constant thought and constant heart-searching, yet seldom rewards you with contented peace and the jackpot of delighted smiles, you may find that you are looking more and more to outside rules for guidance in looking after her. And looking to outside rules means that you are letting space develop between you; asking someone who is not your baby.

Am I doing everything I should?

If you let yourself go looking for outside "rules" for good mothers, so that by following them you can feel confident that you *are* a good mother, you will find them. The rules are embodied in baby-care old wives' tales and manuals and the popular literature, and they will be eagerly offered to you by relatives, friends, and neighbors the moment you admit to the least uncertainty about what you have been doing.

Older mothers have a lot of sensible advice to pass on to younger ones, but if you and your baby are to take the useful bits and ignore the rest, you need to be exercising your own judgment about your own child.

Taken uncritically as a whole, few of the tales will be *exactly* right for your baby because, after all, there has never been a baby exactly like her and there never will be one again.

Some of the tales will be off-beam for you because there has never been a mother just like you before, either.

Some of the tales they tell you will be downright misleading in your particular circumstances.

Some of the tales are cruel. That's a strong word to use of things devoted parents do to beloved babies, but from the babies' viewpoint it is the right word.

Let's look at a few common tales so that you can judge for yourself.

Old wives' tale 1

BABIES CRY TO EXERCISE THEIR LUNGS (so if your baby cries when she doesn't need anything obvious, leave her to it).

Repeated daily in hospitals, clinics, and nurseries worldwide, this has to be one of the most idiotic of all tales. Lungs are actively working from the moment a baby takes his or her first independent breath until the moment of death. They are not made of muscle which can be strengthened by an extra workload, and crying is a nonstarter toward "healthy exercise" when compared with contented kicking. . . .

Does the baby at right look as if she is taking healthy exercise, or does she look as if she is trying to get somebody to do something about something as soon as possible?

The tale has not been dismissed with the scorn it deserves because it provides the ideal way out for people who cannot, or will not, cope with crying babies.

If all those mites in the hospital nursery are just "exercising their lungs," the nurses need not bother with them (unless they are ill), need they? And if your baby is taking healthy exercise, you can leave her to it with a clear conscience, can't you?

Turn your back on the tale, not the baby. She is crying because she needs somebody to do something for her. She may not know what it is. You may not be able to find out what it is. But you can try. By trying you will show her that you care; that you will always listen, try to understand, try to help. By learning that, she will come to feel more comfortable, perhaps not right now, perhaps not even tomorrow, but gradually, as her personality unfolds in your reliable warmth.

Left to cry alone, what must she feel?

Helpless. Frustrated. Overwhelmed, in the end, by whatever was making her cry in the first place.

What lesson could she learn? Only that the sole action she is capable of taking to help herself is useless; the only outside help available for her to depend upon is not dependable. We want her to grow up feeling herself to be a competent person in a manageable world, but we shall not achieve that in this way.

She is not crying to exercise her lungs but to call to you. If you can still let yourself listen to your own feelings, you know it. Don't let old tales distance you from your baby.

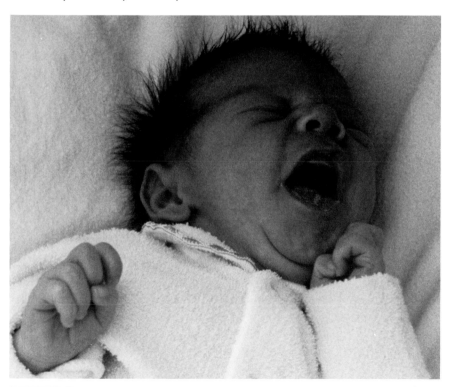

Old *wives' tale* 2

BABIES SHOULD BE FED EVERY FOUR HOURS (so you certainly need not, and probably should not, feed yours more often whatever she "says").

Your baby, like all babies, needs feeding when she feels hungry. Your baby, like all babies, may feel hungry twenty minutes or two, three, or four hours after she was last offered food. Your baby, like all *people*, gets hungrier on some days than on others and eats more at some meals than at others.

This particular tale may be presented to you, very convincingly, as a matter of factual biology. You may be told that it takes about four hours for a baby to digest a full feeding and that to feed yours sooner is to put "new milk on top of old" and risk giving her "indigestion." If you question your adviser closely about the point of waiting *exactly* four hours from meal to meal, she will probably make herself sound very modern and flexible by saying: "Well, of course you don't have to keep watching the clock . . . a few minutes early won't hurt." Don't let that fool you. Her biology is an outdated fake, and you could feed your baby exactly as she needed feeding if you did not have a clock or a watch in the house. Worldwide, most mothers do.

Once upon a time (when today's old wives were very young) *some* babies could be content with the approved routine of four-hourly feeding. They were bottle-fed with milk meant for calves rather than babies; it made such large and indigestible curds in their stomachs that digesting it really did take quite a long time. Your baby of the eighties gets your own milk — or cow's milk which has been so much modified that no calf would recognize it — and she almost certainly starts out by asking for little and often. It's not difficult to understand why. In the womb, she was fed by a continual transfusion from your bloodstream and knew nothing of hunger or of a full or empty stomach. She has to learn about all that; learn to suck until she feels "full" and to stay contented while she gets more and more "empty." Sometimes she cannot stay awake long enough to take all she can hold; sometimes the breast-milk supply is down so that there is less than usual for her to take; and whatever amount of milk she takes, she digests it so easily that she is soon ready for more. Sucking is not only for food, either. She has to suck milk if she is thirsty rather than hungry and she also has to suck for pleasure, comfort, entertainment, love. . . .

Part of the point of satisfactory breastfeeding is to have *all* those things

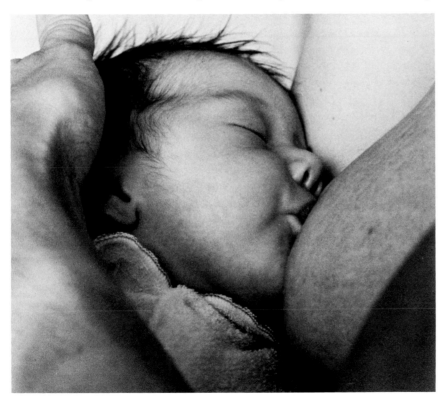

available to your baby, all the time and wherever you are. Why look at a clock? She cannot tell the time.

There are not many (any?) mothers who keep their babies to the letter of this tale, but there are many who feed their babies a reluctant eight times a day for a few weeks and then lose heart and their milk and turn thankfully to bottles and cereals. There are probably even more who do feed their babies as often as the babies want feeding, but who are so guilty about doing so that they never admit to the true count. Concealing the count, like a cigarette smoker, keeps the tale alive, of course. If you knew that almost *every* baby (and mother) disobeyed the "rules," at least in the early weeks, you wouldn't feel so pressured to try to keep to them yourself.

Old wives' tale 3

NEW BABIES SLEEP EIGHTEEN TO TWENTY HOURS IN EVERY TWENTY-FOUR (so if yours does not, you aren't "managing" him properly).

There are (a few) new babies who really do wake to be fed, fall asleep when they are full, and stay that way until they are hungry again. If such a baby had a strong suck and a mother who was efficient at diaper changing and washing, and not given to wasting time on coos and cuddles, he might possibly reach this sleep total. Possibly.

But don't expect it. Most mothers find that feeding, loving, and caring for a baby takes them more than six hours in the twenty-four, irrespective of the baby's behavior. And most babies, right from the beginning, want to be awake sometimes just because they have had enough sleeping for the moment.

Believing this particular tale would not actually lead you to alter your baby's natural behavior because you cannot *make* a wakeful baby sleep when he does not feel like it. But expecting him to sleep, feeling that he *ought* to sleep, can ruin both his play times and your nerves. When he wants to study your face, he wants you to smile and talk to him, not keep saying "Now go to sleep, darling." And when he decides to be awake for a bit, it is far more fun for both of you if his carriage comes into the kitchen, or wherever you want to be, than if you have to keep rushing to soothe him in another room. . . .

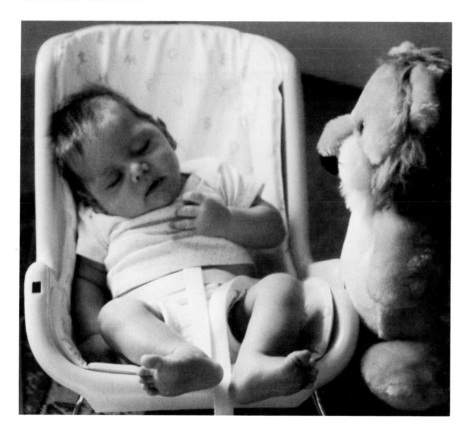

Old wives' tale 4

BABIES SHOULD BE BATHED EVERY DAY (irrespective of what they feel about it).

Being bathed gives many new babies the heebie-jeebies and leaves their mothers in a shower of nervous sweat.

Although a lot of babies enjoy the two minutes they spend actually submerged in warm water, everything else about a bath is designed to terrify them.

They have to have their clothes removed and, while the outer layers may be an opportunity for pleasant chat, the inner layers make many babies increasingly anxious, as if you were removing the last barriers between their supersensitive skins and the big outside world. Your baby may be one of many who begins to cry the moment you start to remove her undershirt, or perhaps one of the infinitely pathetic few who clutches it with desperate fingers. It isn't that these babies get *cold*; they react this way however warm you make the room. It is that they feel exposed. A textured piece of fabric — such as a towel or cellular blanket — laid over the naked tummy usually stops the crying, but did it have to begin?

Naked, or towel-wrapped, the baby has to be washed on your lap and seems to dislike the feeling of cool sticky soap as much as we do. Probably she is held with her head over the edge of the bath while her apology for hair is washed and then she has to be lifted in.

Lovely though it may be for her to find herself half-floating in liquid warmth, head and neck securely supported on your wrist, shoulder safely steadied by your hand, *getting* there arouses all her terror of being dropped. She has only just time to forget those screams and move her legs in the water before she has to go through it all in reverse. She's probably starving, too, since conventionally baths are given before feedings. . . .

A bath achieves nothing extra to a good-enough wash, and you can wash

every bit of your new baby adequately without ever making her feel deprived of her clothes, liable to be dropped, or anything else that she will dislike.

She does not have to have a bath every day. She does not have to have a bath ever. Most of the world's babies do not. There will come a time — perhaps at two months or three — when your baby is ready to enjoy the freedom of nakedness and, because she can support her own head and neck, is no longer so terrified of being dropped. Then you and she can both begin to discover a bath as one of the day's best play-places. Until then, if neither of you enjoys it, you don't have to do it.

Old wives, as well as doctors and other "experts," often know a lot about babies, but they never know anything about your baby. You can make good use of their expertise but only if you put it into the context of your own. If you are tuned in to your baby, involved in her feelings so that you share each spurt of pleasure or flicker of pain, each moment of fear or curiosity, each expression of interest, puzzlement, or need, you will know when outsiders' rules are not right for her.

When the rules are not right for your baby, don't follow them and don't let them bother you. Of course she has to eat and sleep; of course she has to be kept clean. But *how* you arrange these things is up to you — and your baby. Neither her health nor her character demands that you keep her clean by giving her baths which she hates. Looking for another way to accomplish the same end without upsetting her is an important part of personal parenting.

You will not always be able to find trouble-free ways through daily life, of course. Your baby may simply loathe being dressed, for example. Once you have experimented with dressing her on your lap or on a changing table, with doing it before or after her feeding, and with putting her arms in first or her feet in first, you may decide that nothing makes any difference and your baby is just quirky about dressing. She has to *be* dressed, so the sensible thing to do is just to get on with it by whatever method is fastest. You have thought about this minute issue from her point of view. You have put yourself into her nonexistent shoes to look for an answer and this is the best you can do. Fine. You may not have come up with a technique for trouble-free dressing, but you have shared the dressing business with her; you have not simply done what you thought you ought to do, what you were told to do or what everybody does, *irrespective of her feelings*. Even when you dress her against her will and against her yells, you are treating her as a person, not as an object.

7 If being tuned in only deafens you

"I'd do *anything* to stop him crying," says the exhausted and desperate mother.

"It's all very well to talk about meeting babies' needs, doing what they want so as to keep you both happy, but I don't *know* what he wants. He just cries!"

Being tuned in to a baby who is often unhappy is not a cheerful business. Because you are tuned in, you do not only see and hear his misery, you feel it too. What hurts him hurts you, and if he cannot enjoy the sunshine or relax through a lazy afternoon, you certainly cannot.

His crying hurts you in other ways, too. It makes you feel feeble and incompetent, unfit to be a parent. He cries, so you pick him up, but after a moment's pause he cries in your arms. You try to catch his eye but his are screwed up with distress and if you insist on putting your face close up, he may even turn his away. You joggle him and he cries harder; you try to cradle his stiff little body against yours but he fights. You put him down again in his crib and the crying peaks, but when you pick him up *again* it scarcely diminishes. . . .

If a pattern like this is repeated, hour after hour, or evening after evening, the temptation to tune *out* is tremendous. Why should you leave yourself exposed to his pain and to the frustration of your own inability to help him? Inside your head, the baby who *cannot* be comforted tends to turn into a baby who *will not* be comforted. You cannot find out what he really needs, so it is easy to conclude that he doesn't really need anything: "He's just trying it on." Because you feel inadequate and guilty at not being able to help him, you make the whole thing his fault. Do you remember the Red Queen in *Through the Looking-Glass*?

> Speak roughly to your little boy
> And beat him when he sneezes.
> He only does it to annoy
> Because he knows it teases.

Anyone who has ever had to cope with a crying baby whom she loved must sympathize with the Red Queen, but everyone who has to cope with a crying baby whom she loves must guard against being like her.

Your crying baby does not know that he is driving you crazy. He does not know that broken nights are making you feel like a sleepwalker. He doesn't know anything about your feelings because he does not even know that you exist as a separate person from himself. He is crying not to "get at" you, but because he is overwhelmed by his own unhappy feelings. Only you can help him to be happier, so if you tune out in anger you condemn him (and yourself) to more and more crying.

You probably did not begin to feel helpless and infuriated until you had looked for all the obvious causes, and cures, for your baby's unhappiness. You know that he is getting as much as he wants to eat (rather than as much as you had thought he could need) and as often as he will accept it (rather than at the intervals you had thought proper). You have made sure that he is not getting too hot or too cold, that his plastic pants do not cut into him, and that the toddler is not sneaking in to frighten him — or worse. You may even have taken him to the doctor to be certain that he has no physical symptoms of illness. You have done everything you can think of and you are left with a crying baby.

What more *can* you do?

Start by accepting that if you have not been able to find a single cause and cure for your baby's unhappiness, there probably isn't one. He may be one of those babies who is unhappy with the whole business of independent life. Perhaps his nervous system is a bit immature, so that he is especially vulnerable to the sensations of life — its sights and sounds, its textures and feelings, its tastes and smells. Perhaps parts of his nervous system lag behind the rest so that, for example, his own digestive processes, normal in themselves, impinge uncomfortably upon his consciousness instead of staying comfortably below that level. Perhaps he has not yet discovered how to be fully hungry or fully satisfied, so that he often wants food but can seldom be bothered to suck with enthusiasm. Perhaps he has not yet learned to be fully awake or fully asleep, so that he hovers uncomfortably between the two states, too "tired" to be interested and sociable yet too "awake" to relax into slumber. Perhaps. The truth is that we do not *know* what these globally unhappy babies feel. We do not know what makes them cry and therefore what would help them to feel happier.

If there is no single or known cause for your baby's unhappiness, you cannot find one. Realize that your baby's crying is no reproach to you — that it is your burden and not your fault — and you may be able to fend off the guilt which otherwise makes you defensive and angry. Realize also that your baby's unhappiness is his burden and not his fault and you may be able to stay sympathetic and tuned in with him, instead of deciding that he is "a cross kind of baby," "overdemanding," or just "difficult."

Babies who feel like this have to grow through whatever aspects of development are bothering them. Time is on their side because they are changing and growing up with every day that passes. Whether it takes *your* baby three weeks or three months to feel generally better about life he will come through the early miseries which make him look unhappy even in sleep. Be patient and one day soon he will welcome you and the world you represent with irresistible grins.

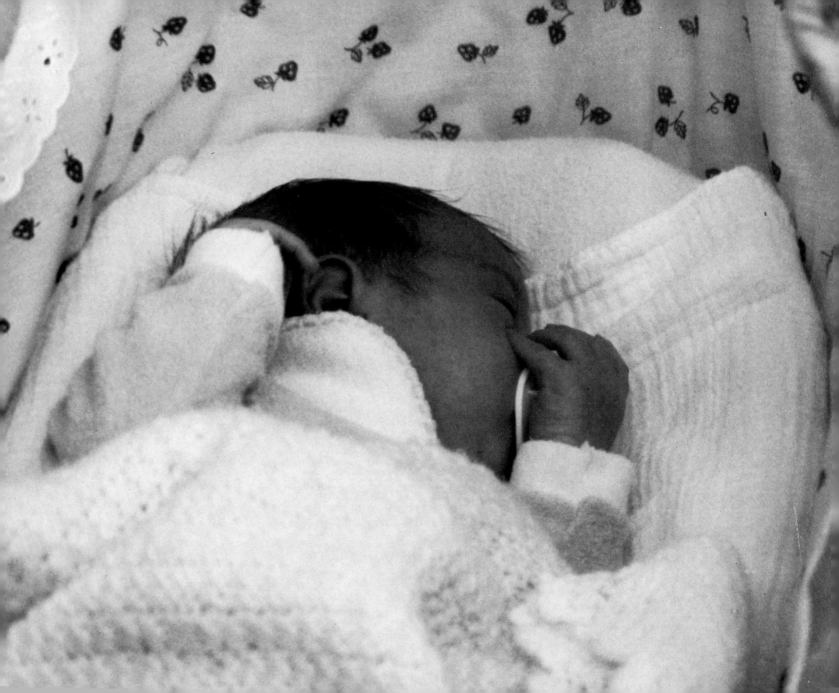

So why not just tune out and let your baby do his own suffering while he does his own growing up? Because you can work with the growing-up process, hold on to your image of yourself as a good and loving parent *and* keep your baby as nearly happy as he is capable of being, *if you will keep experimenting with ways to comfort him* even though no single way works completely or for long. Experiment for long enough and you may even find a solution: not a single comfort which miraculously makes him feel better (you have already tried all of those), but a combination of comforts which work for the moment if you offer them all together.

Combination-comfort may work for your baby if you are certain that he doesn't need any simple, single aid (like food because he's hungry), and if anything you do for him seems to cheer him for a moment, even though nothing cheers him for long.

It seems to work like this: the baby is generally, globally, uncomfortable. If he is crying in his crib, being picked up gives him a change and helps for a moment but then his unhappiness breaks through again. If you wrap him, rock him, sing to him, each new sensation makes another change, another break in his unhappiness, but as he adapts to each one, the discomfort comes through and he cries again. If you can find enough of these small comforts, and pile them all together on top of your baby's uncomfortable feelings, you may actually smother them — for now.

One baby, after a long labor and difficult forceps delivery, was breast-fed but always wakeful and seldom happy for long. His mother tried everything to keep him contented, but instead of settling down during his very first weeks, he became more and more miserable. She became more and more miserable, too. One despairing day she decided to try the one thing she had always been determined not to give her baby. Despite a lifetime's prejudice against them, she gave him a pacifier — and it worked.

The baby took that pacifier and he sucked and sucked as if it was what he had been asking for. He went to sleep and she burst into tears: "If that was all he wanted, why didn't I give him one before?"

It wasn't all he wanted, of course. The pacifier was one more small comfort, but it wasn't a solution, all by itself.

When the baby was really unhappy, he screamed. When he screamed, he could take the pacifier but he could not keep it in his mouth. He wanted to suck but the crying broke through, the pacifier fell out, and its sudden departure gave him yet another misery to cry about. Like all the other comforts she had tried, it looked as if it was a little bit helpful sometimes, but not very helpful most of the time.

The baby liked being held with his stomach pressed against his mother's breast and he liked being walked and danced with. One night she had held him, walked him, danced with him until she was ready to drop with exhaustion. She sank down in what happened to be a rocking chair and discovered, quite by chance, that that movement soothed him even more than her walking and that the TV was distracting him as well. Sitting in the rocking chair with the TV on and the baby pressed against her, she made the final miraculous discovery: in that position the pacifier stayed in the baby's mouth unless he positively spat it out. Peace descended. Between them that mother and baby had arrived at a collection of comforts which worked all together though none worked alone. For a few weeks "going to the rocking chair" was an effective and ritualized response whenever the baby became really distressed. After that, little bits of the ritual began to drop away until he no longer needed all those comforts and an "ordinary cuddle" would do.

The particular combination of cuddling, rocking, sucking, and TV which "worked" for that mother-baby pair might not "work" for you. Parents and babies are individuals. They have to work out individual solutions to their own problems. Her approach might be useful, though.

She hit on her combination-comforts by chance and because she was "trying everything." She hit on them because she was willing to consider *anything*, even the pacifier of which she so much disapproved. And she hit on them because she was trying so hard that her exhaustion and the rocking chair just happened to come together.

If she had tuned out from her crying baby, taking refuge in outside advice ("leave him to cry") or in blaming him ("he's testing you"), he and she would both have had to endure weeks of misery. Those weeks might have left them further apart and less ready to enjoy each other than they were when they gave up the rocking chair.

If you can find combination-comforts which calm and cheer your crying baby, it is not only he who will be happier but both of you. However much time and energy you spend in comforting your baby, no price is too high if it protects you from feeling helpless, useless, and hopeless.

Even if you cannot find a ritual which entirely works, your thinking and watching and trying will still be worthwhile. Your baby may not feel any happier right now, despite everything you can do, but he is not abandoned in his sadness. You may not get any more sleep tonight than you had last night, but at least you know that you are truly doing your best and that what you do for your baby is infinitely more than anyone else could do.

The bad patch will soon be over because your baby is growing up and growing through it. Go through it with him and, when he is ready, he will turn outward to respond to you and to the exciting world you offer.

8 Expanding your growing baby's world

As far as your baby is concerned, you are her completing half. When there is something wrong, you put it right. When she is lonely, you come. When she is hungry, you feed her. When she is tense, you stroke or rock her. You are the restorer of peace and equilibrium.

In her very first days and weeks, this is probably your most vital function. Because she is still new to the outside world, everything about it threatens to upset or unbalance her. You stand between her and that unmanageable world, protecting her so that she can come to terms with it all as peacefully as possible.

But your baby does not stay brand new for long. Tiny though she may still seem when she is six or ten weeks old, she will look positively gross if you then put her alongside somebody whose age is measured in days. Already she has done a great deal of physical growing and a great deal of growing up, too. As she grows up, even this early on, your role as her other half expands.

There begin to be many, many things which she can do *if you will help her*. And many, many things which she will enjoy *if you will show her*.

An increasingly important part of what you can show her is the community which surrounds your home.

You and your baby may have been so taken up with each other during her first weeks of life that the outside world seemed to go out of focus for you. You had to go out, of course, for the shopping if for nothing else, but sharp-focus reality may have seemed confined to the home-nest where you were helping your baby to start being a person.

Sooner or later (and which it is probably rather depends upon the time of year), you are going to remember that outside world and begin to want to get back into it. You will not be going out as you were before, though. You need a welcome which extends to your baby, too.

In a small town or the kind of street which feels itself to be a community, parents may get a real welcome the first time they push their baby out to show her off. One mother described it like this:

> We'd been living in this tiny village while I was pregnant but then we had to go away for three months, during which the baby was born. When we came back, *everybody* wanted to see her and wherever we went people automatically made room for her pram. The man who owned the pub even moved tables over so that we could still sit in our old corner. It gave me a tremendous sense of the continuity of everything. I'd gone away waddling, with my bulge taking up enough room for two. When I came back I was two and everybody knew it and welcomed it. . . .

Of course every community *ought* to feel like that about new parents and babies because those babies are the community's future. Sadly, though, they do not always seem to know it.

If your home area is part of a big impersonal city or the kind of new town or development where people seem to try *not* to know each other, you may find that nobody "outside" seems to know or care about your divinely beautiful, brilliantly intelligent, and totally miraculous baby. You may even find that you-and-she as a pair are far less desirable customers and citizens than you were when she was still inside.

Cities today are planned (insofar as they are planned at all) for wage earners with cars. As a new person's other half, you are likely to be on foot with a stroller. The cars and trucks do not just take up the whole road, they park with two wheels on the sidewalk and open their doors into your baby's face. They park on the diagonal so you cannot see to push the stroller safely over pedestrian crossings, and they choke every inch of your route to the nearest park or mall.

Nobody seems worried about making your pedestrian life so difficult. On the contrary, the fact that your stroller takes up space on the narrow sidewalks will earn you glares from people who have *important* things to do, while if you cannot get across the road fast enough to suit that taxi, the driver will often honk more willingly than he brakes.

If strolling about is not much of a pleasure — and nobody is admiring your lovely baby anyway — doing the jobs you came out to do can be tricky, too. Supermarkets will let you push your stroller around (they can hardly pretend there's no room when they have those shopping carts, can they?), but smaller stores often say "No strollers" and leave you to work out a solution. I wonder whether they really expect you to leave your baby outside to be rained on, jostled, even stolen? Or do they expect you to go through the business of unharnessing her and taking her out so that you can have the pleasure of carrying her with one arm, your purse with the other arm, and your shopping with — the third?

Your baby has needs and you are in the business of meeting them. But even that entirely private matter may not be straightforward in public. In most places you will not actually be "told off" for breastfeeding, but you will be "looked at" and they will not be glances of shared contentment, either. Should some other need arise — a change of diaper, for instance — you are on your own. "They" either don't know or they don't care. Either way, only that rarity the "mother's room" will offer any help.

Brace yourself.

Don't apologize unless you actually run someone over with that stroller.

You and your baby have at least as much right to get out and about and use any facilities the area offers as anybody else.

She cried in the library? Tut-tut. The sound will not actually *hurt* them (her crying only hurts you), and that library belongs to you. You are a taxpayer, after all.

She threw up in the café? Oh dear. Every single person in that café used to throw up too, and, what is more, most of them have children of their own who do it. They are only pretending that your baby is an amazingly dreadful phenomenon because, wearing their wage earners' hats, they feel superior.

She threw an apple on the floor of the shop? Clever her.

Even when nobody is actually horrible to you, getting out and about with a baby can seem amazingly difficult. The errand you would have run in ten minutes in pregnancy can take an hour or more now, and an hour of effort, too. You have to get the baby ready and think what you might need for her (a bottle? a diaper? her pacifier? an extra sweater?). You have to organize the stroller (safety harness? rain-protection?). You may have to get both baby and stroller down in an elevator (is it working?) or down stairs. Once you have started out on foot, you are committed to staying on foot because leaping on and off buses is out of the question. If you want to go inside somewhere where you can't take the stroller, you have to find somewhere safe to leave it. If you want to bring anything home, you have to carry it, and if the baby gets cross, passers-by will look at you as if you had made her cry on purpose.

A lot of women feel "stuck in the house" when their children are very young, and no wonder. Getting out is difficult; being out is not rewarding, but staying in is boring and claustrophobic. You can't change your community into the welcoming place it ought to be, but you may be able to change your haunts and your habits so that you have places to go where you do feel welcome and can mostly avoid the places where you do not. If you have to buy bread and could use a lot of other things, a walk to the local bakery could make a pleasant afternoon excursion while a trip to the supermarket would be hell. Don't try to put them together. Take the baby to the bakery, showing her everything along the way and letting it all take the time it takes. Fix the supermarket trip for a different time when your partner can come or when you and a friend can take a car and suffer together. If you are finding your community unwelcoming, other parents will be feeling the same. Where are they? Find them and you will have found a welcoming focus for both you and your baby — and perhaps the beginning of park-seat friendships which can last for years.

That outside world is still more important to you than to your baby, though. She needs you to feel easy and accepted wherever you go, and to have friends who share your interests. But she needs all that because she needs a contented mother. Most of her own needs and developments are still private ones to be made and practiced with you alone. She needs to manage her body before she can make use of the outside world.

Managing her body is a large part of what she's concentrating on now.

Babies' heads have to be large and heavy in proportion to the rest of their bodies because they have to house very large brains. Babies need those large brains so that they can be learning during the early months when bodies and limbs are growing.

So your baby's potential brain power is ahead of his body power. He can see and hear and feel and taste and smell things, and learn about them, but he cannot make opportunities for himself to do so because that heavy head anchors him.

He has to rely on you to support his head and arrange his body in such a way that he *can* do interesting things. And he has to rely on you to give him opportunities to practice managing his head and body so that he can take charge of it himself at the first possible moment.

Giving your baby opportunities takes tact, of course. When you first put him down to "play" on his tummy on the floor, he may not be very

pleased. He can *turn* his head, so as not to smother, but as long as his legs are still bent up under him, he can't *lift* it so he can't look around. If he lies there and cries, he's not learning anything. Nobody can learn when they're miserable. But if he's ready to be interested in that kind of floor-play, he'll soon discover how to straighten his legs out behind him . . . and as he straightens out, his neck muscles will gradually strengthen so that his head can come up.

Your baby will teach himself these tiny but vital new achievements whether you help him or not. Working at growing up is built into him and you could only *stop* him learning by denying him opportunities: keeping him wrapped up in a crib all day, for example. But your baby will teach himself faster and more happily if you will play his games with him. Down on the floor and face to face, it is his desire to look at you which stimulates him to take charge of that heavy head.

Your baby cannot do very much for herself yet. But you can do a great deal to keep her interested and happy if you will think up entertainments for her that *are* within the limits of her physical abilities.

Even if she cannot lift her head very high yet, she can look at all kinds of interesting things if you will put them close beside her.

Even if she can't do much more than lie about, you can provide her with lots of different lying-about experiences from furry rugs to summer grass.

And when she is tired of trying to manage her own body; tired of trying to do things that are at the limits of her strength, you can lend her your body and your strength.

Your baby will not remain a helpless spectator for long.

He is looking, listening, learning, every single day.

He is growing and getting stronger, too.

And he is coming to terms, and making his own terms, with you, his special people, and with the world you all share.

Almost every day he will make a new sound, manage some new physical effort like rolling over, or change his pattern so that instead of always dropping to sleep at the breast he starts to stay awake to look at you, or even drop the nipple (on the second side!) to have a chat. Some parents say that healthy, cheerful babies at this stage of life grow up so fast that it is difficult to keep up with them. As one mother put it: "I was forever wishing I'd offered him that toy last week because whatever I gave him he always seemed ready for that and for something more."

The ideal — for all of you — is to offer new activities and games, things to play with and expeditions, rhymes, songs, and routines, at *exactly* the moment when a baby is first ready to enjoy them.

But of course that's impossible.

The best you can possibly do is spend enough time watching your baby, playing with him, talking to him, listening to him, that you see pretty quickly when he is ready for something fresh.

The worst thing you can do is to look in a book which gives the ages at which babies *ought* to do things, try to make your baby do them, find that he won't, can't, or does not want to, and then decide that he is "slow."

The ages such books give are based on averages and, like all other averages, they have to include babies who do certain things exceptionally early and babies who do those particular things exceptionally late. Once those very different ages have all been added together and divided by the number of babies being studied, you have an "average age" — but it is most unlikely that that average will be very meaningful when it is applied to an individual baby.

So take statements about the ages at which babies do things very cynically indeed unless the book also gives you some idea of the *range of ages* which went into that average figure.

If a range is given, so that it says, "In the next couple of months," or, "Average age 3 months, age-range 6 weeks to 4½ months," don't be like

the mother who solemnly listened to an explanation of that kind of average and range, then said: "Yes, I do understand. I know that perfectly normal babies do this at 6 weeks, or 8 weeks, or 12 weeks, or 16 weeks. . . . I'd just like my baby to be one of the 6-week ones, that's all."

Your baby's development is a process, not a race.

It is very important to his happiness (and yours) that you understand that. Development unfolds from inside him, helped by you, his other special people, and the life you provide for each other, but nothing whatsoever to do with the development of any other baby.

There is no "right age" for him to do anything, other than the age at which it becomes right for *him*: manageable, enjoyable, something for which he is ready.

Other people will certainly say things to you like: "Isn't he sleeping through yet? Mine's been sleeping through since she was six weeks," or: "He's in no hurry to sit up, is he? You sat *very* early as a baby." Do try not to listen.

All human babies develop along the same road from birth to being grown up, and all babies have to pass the same "milestones" along that road. But no two babies travel at the same pace as each other. And no single baby travels at the same pace all the way.

So if you try to compare your baby with your neighbor's baby of the same age, one of them is absolutely bound to be "ahead" of the other on any particular achievement. But if your baby is ahead of her on, say, rolling over, the chances are that she will be ahead of him on something quite different like smiling.

And if your baby seems to be going much faster than her (or than the "average") right now, that does not at all mean that he is going to carry on at that pace. He may race ahead physically and learn to sit up alone very early, but then be content to stay sitting (while he does lots of other kinds of developing, to do with using his hands or "talking") while she "catches

up" with him by learning to sit and then "overtakes" him by learning to crawl.

And if you should appear to have a baby who really is an exceptionally fast developer in almost every way, even *that* will not mean that he is going to "stay ahead" and grow into an unusually bright child. It is impossible to predict the general intelligence of a *child* from his or her development as a *baby*.

The "developmental assessments" which your doctor may carry out two or three times in the first year are designed to pick out the very, *very* few babies who have real problems. If the doctor says your baby is "doing fine," you can be quite sure that he is, even if he is always the last of all the babies you know to do anything new. His pace is his business; fitting what his environment offers him to that pace is yours. The better you get to know him and the more notice you take of his minute activities, the better you will be able to do it.

Watch what he does with his hands, for instance.

At the beginning he does very little. His hands are not like human hands at all because they are closed into tight little fists almost all the time. While they are closed, you can put your finger in so that the baby "holds on," if you want to, but he will not do anything deliberately with his hands; he is not ready.

When he starts to keep his hands open most of the time, though, you will know that those hands are getting ready for action.

They go to his mouth and get waved around.

And if he is one of those fortunate babies who can suck his thumb with pleasure and satisfaction, instead of needing the breast or a bottle or a pacifier for all his sucking, it is about now that he will perfect the art.

He may even seem to *do* things with his hands by now, like using them to hold his feet up while he sucks his toes. But don't be fooled into thinking that he's ready for elaborate toys. He isn't really *using* his hands yet

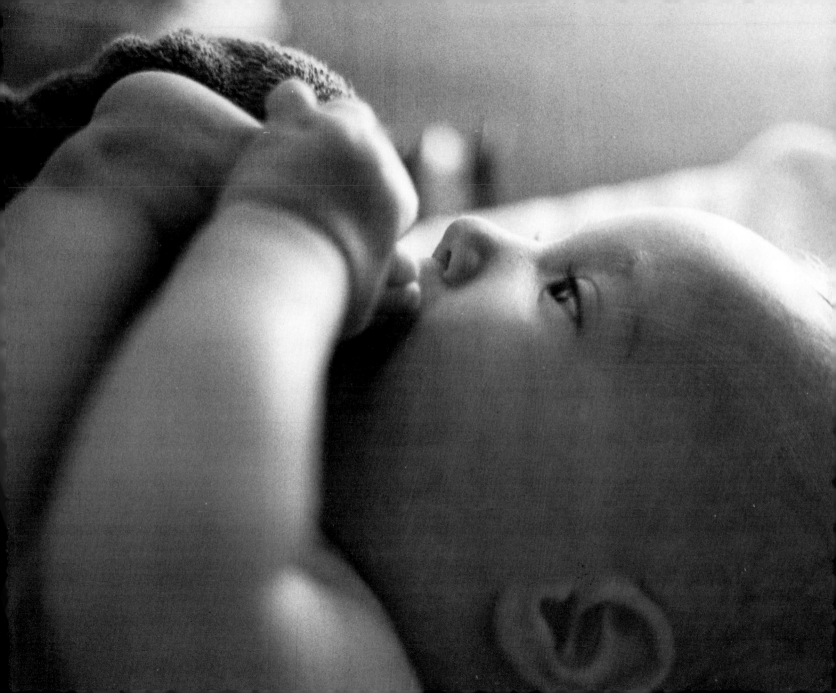

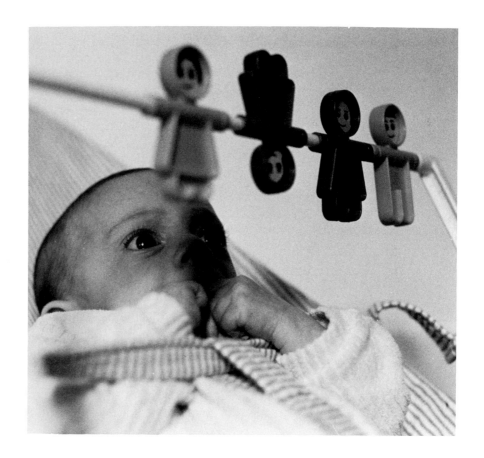

because he does not know he's got them: he hasn't caught sight of them, noticed them, and discovered that they belong to him.

He looks and looks and *looks* at people and objects, but he cannot *do* anything about the things he sees until he has discovered those hands.

This is the stage when rattles really come into their own. Your open-handed baby can grasp a rattle and, as she waves her arms around, it makes a noise.

The sound attracts her attention. She looks toward it and what does she suddenly see? The rattle *in her hand*.

Whether she first "notices" her own hand with a rattle's help, or just by chance as it passes across her line of sight in its random wavings, your baby will soon afterward realize that her hands are *always there* and that she can make them do things, make them come and go, bring them together and separate them, put them in her mouth and then take them out again for inspection, and even make the fingers work separately.

Once a baby finds her own hands, by eye as well as by touch and mouth, they are her very best toys and on their way to being her most useful tools, too, when she can get them organized for reaching out and grabbing.

9 Beginning to know that you are you

While you are showing your baby things and calling his attention to more and more interesting experiences in his new world, you are also drawing his attention to the most interesting things of all: yourselves.

As his parents, you have of course been vital to him from his very beginning. You "designed" him by bringing that particular sperm and egg together. No other couple could have made this particular baby, and even the two of you could not have made the *same* baby by making love on another occasion. You "grew" him; you brought him into the world, and you gave him the care which he had to have if he was to survive and go on growing outside your body. So from your points of view he has been your very own baby for a long time now.

The baby's point of view is different, though. The blood-tie which may be an important part of your feelings for your child means nothing to him. His interest in your faces and voices was apparent very soon after he was born, but he was not interested in you because you were his parents or because you were yourselves, but because interest in adults was part of his survival kit. Where your early croons and cuddles were personally directed at him (and perhaps would not have been offered to any other baby), his crying and — later on — his enchanting smiles were directed at any responsive adult who came within his range. If you received most of them, that was because you were the adults who *were* within range; but if you had handed the baby to somebody else, he would have interacted with that "stranger" just as he did with you. He did not "know" that the world contained many different adults. He did not "know" that some of them were specially related to him. He probably did not even realize that his body had definite limits and that everybody outside those limits was separate from himself. Tiny babies are, as far as we know, only aware of themselves and their own sensations. They are so completely unaware of the difference between "self" and "not self," that they will suck their own hand or an adult's hand and can be swapped from one to the other without noticing the change.

If a new baby's survival only requires suitable adult care, that same baby's development as a human being requires individual relationships; special two-way relationships. You have been offering your baby your side; he is now ready to move toward offering his. He is ready to notice the differences between people and, once he has done that, he will be quick to choose the people who are to be "special" to him.

Parents often don't notice their beloved baby falling in love with them, and that is a pity because earning a baby's real, passionate love must be one of life's most rewarding experiences, let alone the best part of being somebody's parent.

Some just take it for granted. They love the baby; the baby clearly loves them. Why not?

Some do indeed notice the baby becoming more and more passionate about them but put it down to "cupboard love." The baby gets hungry or thirsty, and they provide food/drink. He gets bored, so they provide entertainment. He cries, so they comfort him. Such parents believe that the baby only loves them for what he can get from them, and that is sad as well as untrue.

Some notice the difference between the baby's behavior with them and with "strangers" and assume that the difference is due to his dislike of the other people rather than his special liking for them. That's sad, too, and certainly not true in this first half year of a new life.

So how can you tell when your baby is beginning to know you as different from other people?

You will pick up the earliest signs if you consider your baby when he is with one of you *and* somebody else. If you and a visitor go to his crib when he announces that it is time for a late-evening feeding, for example, and you both hang over the crib so that your faces are the same distance from his as he lies on his back, he will almost certainly stop crying because somebody has come (and he already knows that that means help), and he will then look at your two faces, one by one, carefully examining them from eyes to chin to hairline and back to eyes. If he only smiles at one face, it will be yours. If he smiles at both, you will be able to tell whether there is any difference in those smiles: once he knows you are you, "your" smile will come quicker and be bigger and "smilier" than the stranger's.

If he is crying too much to stop and look (let alone smile) at anybody, being picked up by the stranger may stop him, but if it does not, he may stop when you take him.

If you are out with your baby at a store, and he is sitting happily in the crook of your arm, he may willingly allow himself to be taken and admired by a stranger, but if he knows that you are you, he will come back to you with smiles and coos and probably grasp your hair. And if you are sitting in your own living room with the baby happily ensconced on a visitor's lap, you will see the difference in his feelings for you and for him very clearly when you take him back. He was perfectly happy and sociable with him, but he treats your body as if it belonged to him and helps himself to bits of your face.

So it is not that your two- or three- or four-month baby does not like strangers and therefore reacts with relief to you who are familiar. He is still perfectly happy to be sociable with anybody who will be sociable with him. It is that *you are beginning to be the very best.*

Try to accept the compliment and don't denigrate your own baby by calling it "cupboard love." It truly is not. Of course, it is important to babies to be fed and kept safe and comfortable, but they repay that kind of care in physical growth and well-being, not in love. You earn a baby's love by ensuring his emotional growth and well-being; by talking to him, listening and responding when he "talks" to you; noticing and smiling when he "catches your eye"; and holding, cuddling, and caressing him. When all those kinds of caring go on together, with mother, father, and perhaps a caretaker all chatting and smiling, playing and cuddling while they give feedings or change diapers, the baby experiences his whole world and all his special people as loving and lovable. But if circumstances demand that the baby's care be divided up, so that one adult takes overall charge of his daily care while others' roles are limited to social times in the evenings and on weekends, the baby will still tend to love most those who socialize most. That is why fathers who take no part in baby care but enjoy an evening play hour can still be specially beloved—sometimes to the chagrin of mothers who spend all day caring for the household and find themselves supplanted as soon as their partners come home. But it is also why a mother who returns to work outside the home, leaving her baby with a caretaker, can be assured that her relationship with the baby need not suffer just because she is not there all day and does not get the meals or keep the house in order with her own hands.

Babies give no credit for the time adults spend away from them, doing chores or working for money. What matters to them is their interaction with adults. While the concept of "quality time" is sometimes overstretched to suggest that parenting can be packed into half an hour's concentrated attention a day, it is certainly true that a baby who is warmly cared for by *somebody* through the working day and truly enjoyed by one or both parents the rest of the time will love them no less for the hours spent apart.

The real threat to parents' places in their baby's affections is lack of time for *personalized* loving attention. However completely parents devote themselves to their baby for the hour or so between their arrival home from

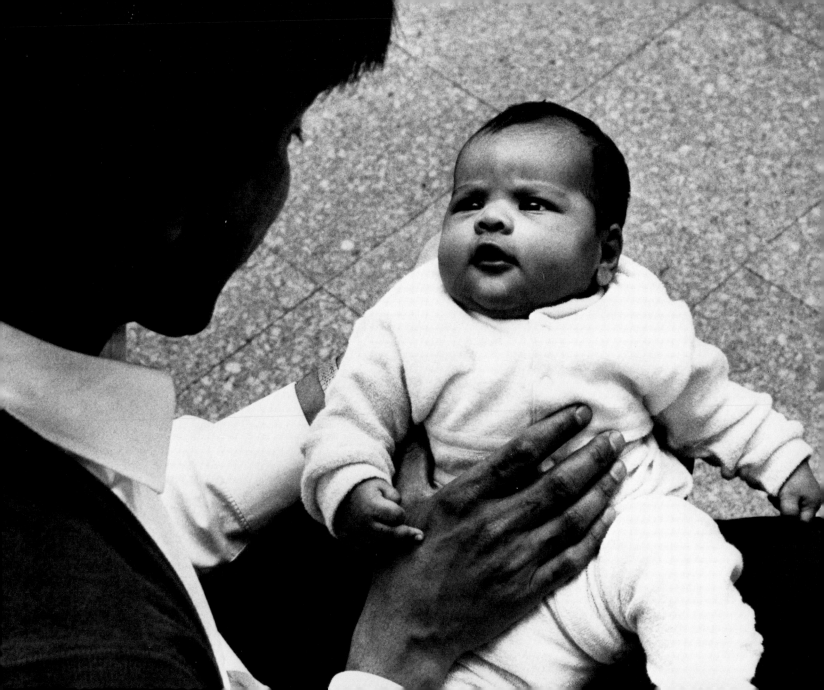

work and the baby's sleeptime, it can be difficult for them to pick up the mood of the day and the moment; to keep in touch with the baby's daily development and generally "tune in" as they open the door. It can be done, and many parents manage it, especially if the caretaker will give an instant bulletin about matters which concern the baby's feelings ("Her teeth are driving her mad, but she's got a passion for this wooden spoon") rather than confining herself to a formal report about matters concerning physical well-being, such as meals eaten and hours slept. Every couple and every single parent has to work these things out as best they can in their individual circumstances, but it is usually worth remembering that a baby's point of view — and especially her view of life's priorities — is likely to be different from yours.

She loves people whom she knows as loving, responsive, and fun. She is quite incapable of loving anyone for all the work they do for her or for earning the money to buy her nice toys. She does not actually care whether her diapers are whiter-than-white or whether her dinner is home-cooked or out of a jar. She does not even care about smart new rattles and stuffed animals as long as she can have lots of spoons and lids and plastic cups to play with and a soft piece of material to cuddle when she can't have mom or dad. So while every parent must decide how to live, what his or her priorities are and how to allocate time, nobody should be allowed to get away unchallenged with statements like "I work my fingers to the bone for that baby." Whoever is caring for her, her ideal would be to have all of them work for her less and play with her more.

Nobody need ever be jealous of a baby's love for somebody else, either. That love is not rationed; there is no limited supply to be shared by all the people who would like some. On the contrary, a baby's love feeds upon itself so that the more she is giving out and receiving, the more she will give out (and therefore receive). A devoted mother who is at home with the baby all day will not deprive the devoted but often-absent father of that baby's love but ensure that she is a loving baby who will respond to him with joy when she has the chance. An affectionate nursery teacher or babysitter who takes care of a baby while his mother works will not take some of the love which was due to her, either, but will help him to grow up loving and lovable by standing in for the mother when she cannot be there.

So earning your small baby's love is not in any sense a competition. And it is not something at which you can fail, provided that you *do* love your baby and that you can make sure the baby knows it.

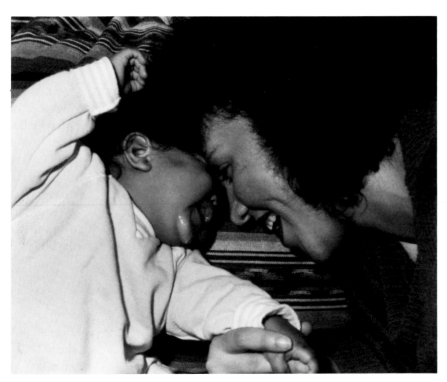

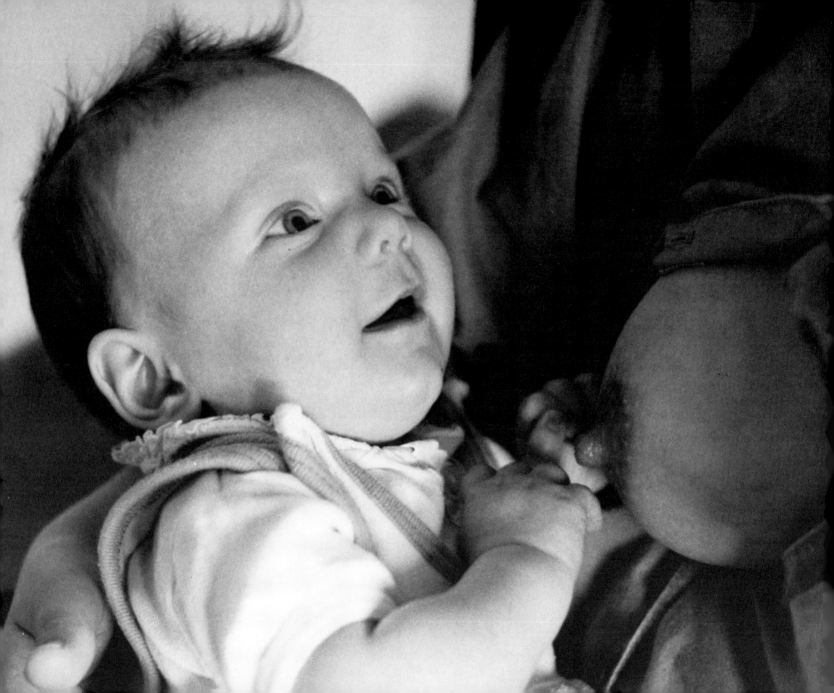

10 Beginning to take an active part in the world

When your baby was brand new, he probably did not want to have much to do with the huge and complicated world into which he had suddenly been pushed. He needed you to create a small and manageable world-within-a-world for him: a setting where, protected from most other people and outside events, he could come to terms with you and with his own newly separated body.

As he settled down, though, you probably felt him developing confidence and interest, day by day, until the small world of feeding and sleeping, of being changed and dressed, washed and petted, cuddled, rocked, and put to sleep again, got boring. He worked at getting control of his body and his limbs, and he needed you to make opportunities for him and lend him your body to make up for the weaknesses of his. He learned more and more about the world by looking at the faces and the objects you brought for him to see, and you and he got better and better at understanding each other.

Now your baby is going to begin to want to *do something about it all*. He was not born to be a passive receiver and observer of life but an active participant, and as soon as he is ready for even the minutest pieces of independent action, he needs you to help and encourage him.

It may sound absurd to talk of "independent action" in a baby who is perhaps only three or four months old. It is not, though. If you imagine yourself after a severe stroke, totally paralyzed and helpless, unable to express your needs, move your body, do *anything* to relieve your own discomforts or fearful boredom, you will have some idea of the helplessness of the newborn. Now imagine that little tiny bits of recovery were taking place so that one day you found that you could close your lips to signal "No more of that revolting food you are trying to spoon into me," or turn your head a little to relieve the discomfort of a crumpled ear. Wouldn't those minute abilities mean a real return of at least some kind of independent control over your own fate? Wouldn't they be overwhelmingly important? Of course new babies are not the same as stroke victims because, unlike those stricken adults, they have no expectations of healthy adult activity. But it is still not a bad parallel to have in the back of your mind if you want to avoid being one of the many parents who, quite without meaning to, bully and bore their babies.

Helping your baby toward independence

Your baby's "independence" does not just arrive, overnight, when he becomes capable of doing something entirely for himself. It builds, from the time that he is settled into the world outside the womb, through your listening to his "messages" about what he wants and does not want; your readiness to help when he shows that he wants to have a go at something; and your willingness to let him make his own tiny decisions.

A lot of early "messages" are given through crying and smiling, but babies use subtler signals, too.

If your baby closes his mouth and turns his head away from the nipple, you know that he does not want any more milk for the moment. He cannot scramble off your lap, hurl the bottle across the room, or even fight you off with his hands. But he is telling you: "Enough (for now)." If you try to persuade him to go back to sucking, you are refusing to receive that message, refusing to "listen," and therefore denying him the right to control his own milk intake or the pace and timing of his feeding.

Before long your baby's desire to have this kind of control—to feed *himself* rather than *being fed*—will probably become much clearer. He may use his newly efficient hands to "take charge of" the breast, treating it as his, rather than yours. If you still tried to feed him with his hands snugly wrapped in a shawl and out of the way, he'd fight, and be quite right to.

The more confident a baby becomes in the recurrent bliss of feeding, the more casually he will take it. He may even use his hands to push himself off the nipple with a nice popping sound and then look to you to share the joke. Feeding need not be all serious business once a baby can take charge of it.

Being fed from a spoon does make babies feel very helpless, especially if it starts before they have found much use for their hands. After all, feeding has meant sucking up to now, and although babies can suck food *off* a spoon, somebody else controls the rate at which the spoonfuls reach them as well as controlling their contents. When a baby is used to nothing but milk, it must be amazing to be offered apple or cereal. And even when he is used to some different foods, it must be dreadfully frustrating not to be able to say, "I want a spoonful of *that*, not *that*, and I think strained carrots are revolting today."

If solid foods are delayed for a few months, babies can participate from the beginning as long as parents and caretakers realize that it is better for a baby *to eat* than *to be fed*, and that the mess is a small price to pay for eager independence.

The baby with the orange segment abandoned dish-and-spoon eating very early, in favor of fingers-for-everything. His mother tried to give him "suitable finger-foods," but he wanted to try almost everything he saw other people eating and even his mistakes never put him off his food. They were *his* mistakes; part of his exploration of the world rather than horrible tastes someone else had dumped in his protesting mouth.

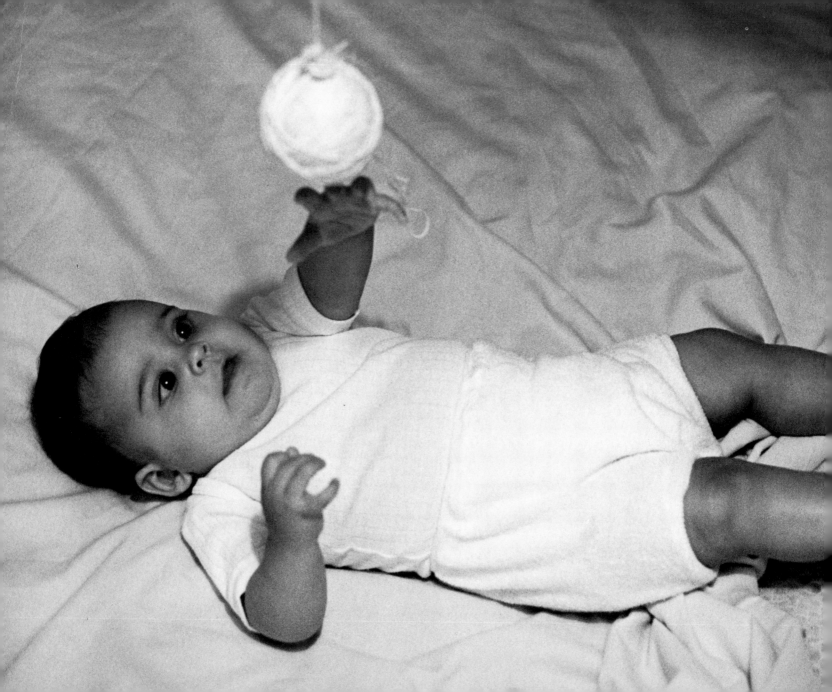

Most of your baby's earliest learning took place through looking and listening: taking in the things she saw and heard but not doing much about them.

Now she wants to join in with the activities she sees around her and wants to have a go at altering things; making them over; or at least getting hold of them.

Sometimes this kind of development does seem to take place overnight, and it can catch parents off guard by putting a baby into danger. Everybody knows that a baby can suddenly learn to roll over and take himself off the edge of his changing table or the top of the stairs, but this little girl had always sat on her mother's lap and watched her drink her morning coffee. Nobody realized that all her play with her hands, her watching of her hands as they waved about with rattles and other toys, had given her the idea of reaching out for things, until it was almost too late. . . .

Of course babies can't be allowed to reach for hot coffee, knives, pencils, or the cat. But once they have the idea of using their hands, they have the key to independent action, and the more they can experience their own power over objects, power to make things happen, the better.

There's a lot of learning involved.

The baby has to learn to focus on something she wants to get hold of; get her hands up to it without fisting them before they get there; get the hands around the object and keep them closed while she brings it back to her for action — which, after all that effort, is probably sucking!

Look at the effort, the sheer concentration, of these babies, each at a different stage in independent action.

This one is only just getting her distance right so her parents have hung a ball over her crib and her whole attention is on touching it. It's a particularly satisfactory game because every time she actually manages to make her hand touch the ball, it will swing. Think of the power: "I do this and *that* happens."

This one has made an amazing discovery. He can not only get hold of the bear, he can actually get the ribbon off. He won't do anything with it, of course, except explore it by putting it in his mouth, but he got it, all by himself, and that's independent action.

All those small adventures were made possible by parents. They were pieces of independent action for the babies, but they all needed some forethought and a bit of scene-setting. A baby who can bash a hanging ball can't hang it up. A baby who can work out how to lean forward has to be propped up first. A baby can't take off a ribbon if there is no ribbon, or if the ribbon that is there is in a knot.

Arranging independent adventures is a big part of your job now, and part of your fun, too. With eyes, hands, and brain all working together, life is full of amazing discoveries if only you will put her in the way of them.

This thing is nice to hold . . .

But it moves . . .

And now it's gone.

Even though babies work so hard at learning by looking and then at getting hold of things that they see, most work even harder at learning to manage their own bodies and then at getting ready to sit, crawl, and stand. Your baby has got to make her body do what she wants it to do. Without that basic independence and control she would remain dependent and more or less passive forever. You cannot *teach* her to roll over or sit up, to get into crawling position, or to get moving, but she depends totally on the opportunities that you give her and on your understanding of today's needs.

Your baby's play is her equivalent of your work. It earns her development just as your work earns you money, and it is just as important to her emotionally as your job is to you.

It is easy to spoil that play; easy to spoil it in the name of her safety and well-being, too.

Watch her on the floor. She can get her feet to her mouth. She wants to suck her toes because sucking things is one of her main ways of finding out about them, but how can she explore her toes if they are always encased in stretch suits or bootees or socks? Such a small point, but so easy to miss.

When she is on her tummy, she has gradually discovered that she can push her head up not just on her elbows but on her hands. She can do it all by herself and for herself, just when she wants to; but she can only do it if you will put her on the floor in the first place.

There are other lovely games to be played when she is on the floor on her tummy, like this airplane game. Balancing *on* her tummy, with both hands and feet off the floor, seems to be a preparation for learning to get her tummy *off* the floor for crawling.

But lying that way up has snags. It is from that position that babies learn to roll all the way over, which is amazingly clever if a bit surprising.

But once she has rolled onto her back, she may be as stranded as an upside-down turtle, bored with that baby stuff called "kicking" and desperate for somebody to come and turn her over or prop her up.

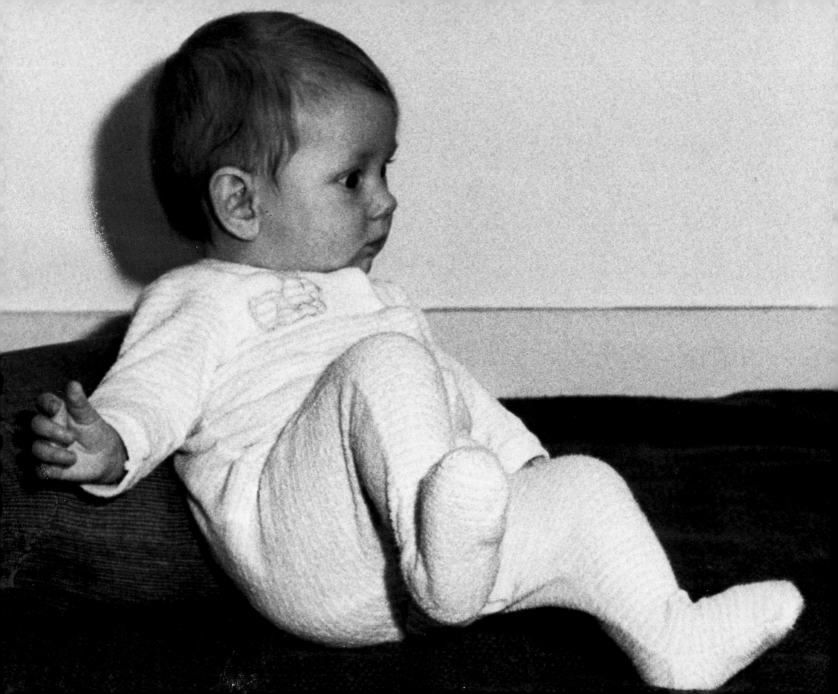

11 *The joys and sorrows of being half a year old*

Around your baby's half birthday, it might be a good idea to take a look at him and at yourselves and take stock of what has been happening to you and where you have got to.

You've had this baby for six months (only *six months*), and already he has changed you both: changed your lives and personalities, your relationships with your families and with each other, and your feelings about all kinds of things from proper wheelchair access to nuclear disarmament. He has dug himself in so that it is difficult to remember what things were like before he emerged, and almost impossible to remember what you thought being a parent was going to be like, except that you didn't expect it to be like this.

The joy of being around a half-year-old is that many things begin to come together for your baby so that with almost every day that passes she finds something new that she can do, or a new way to combine two activities, or a new challenge to set herself — or you.

Today, she may discover that the lovely shrieking noise she has sometimes heard herself make by mistake when you were tickling her is within her own control. She can shriek on purpose, and it is a triumph. She will shriek a lot.

Tomorrow or next month, she may find that if someone will sit her up she can balance — sort of.

But once she can sit she can also fall, and that's scary even when it

doesn't really hurt. Real tears now, not just those baby "wahs" you have got used to. You will mind, all over again, when she cries, and there may be quite a lot of crying to come, one way or another.

In a couple of months the rolling-squirming stuff (which has probably already given you heart failure by taking her from one side of the room to the other when your back was turned) will turn into some kind of crawling, even if it isn't this perfect hands-and-knees kind. Now at last she can go (almost) anywhere she wants and get hold of all the things she has been eyeing and which you (oddly enough) have never brought to her. She has always wanted a good look at the cat's dinner and that electric plug and now she can get there — can't she?

Luckily she is very easy to distract, so you can easily turn her attention to "proper" toys. But because she is so easy to distract, you will not be able to *keep* her attention on proper toys. She will want a go at anything and everything, and that includes the cat's dinner and that electric plug.

Even when she will play "properly," things do behave appallingly badly for her. She puts all that effort into crawling two crawls to get to that truck to take out the person, and what happens? It's enough to put her in a temper for a whole minute, even if you do drop everything to come and help her.

Before a person can begin to learn to sort things out and put them together, she has to muddle them up and empty them out; at last she's got her hands and arms and spine under enough control to manage it. Waste paper baskets and shopping bags, purses and ashtrays, coffee mugs and flower pots . . . as far as she is concerned, they are meant for upending. Her increasing weight and strength helps, too. She has known for ages that something interesting happens when you pull those knobs and now, at last, the cupboard door or that drawer will open for her.

There's a lot of new fun to be had out of throwing things, too. Letting go of things took a lot of learning (fingers which are closed around something

are quite difficult to open when you are very small), but once you can do it there's no end to it. Spoons can be dropped off highchairs (and if there's cereal in them the splat is interesting, too); toys can be thrown out of cribs (though you do have to shout for mom to give them back before there's any question of going to sleep); while the shopping from the cart can leave a lovely trail all the way out of the supermarket.

There probably will not be much peace when you get home, either. Who wants to sit in her own chair and have her own snack when she can sit on mom and have hers? You aren't even going to get that tomato if she knows anything about it. . . .

Then of course there is outright wickedness (or very, very, funny jokes, depending whose point of view you are looking from).

Your baby will know by now that when you say "no," you mean something. *What* you mean or why you mean it is still quite beyond her; but if you say "no" and she goes on doing whatever it was, she knows that you will say it again and that eventually you will do something, like take it away or swoop her up.

That means that she can *make* you do that, just by going on doing the "no" thing, and that can be a game as deliciously funny as peek-a-boo. . . .

It's easy for us to laugh at that mischievous face, but will you be able to?

Those are going to be some of your baby's joys and sorrows. The question is, are they going to be yours, too? Is her pleasure going to give you enough pleasure to counterbalance the strain of constant vigilance for her safety; constant help and comfort when things will not go right; constant demands that you share the amazing discoveries she is making and the stress of occasional broken eggs?

If you feel that she is part of you; that you and she share a life which, when you are together, is largely devoted to her playing, her learning, her growing up, then you will probably be all right because this is what she feels. She has selected you as her "special person" or one of her "special

people." She loves you with passionate and uncritical devotion; she wants you all the time and all to herself; she cannot ever have too much of you, get bored by you, or wish that you were different, and *she is not capable of understanding that you might feel differently.* She cannot understand that you might want "a minute to yourself" because although she may tolerate such minutes in her carriage, she would never choose them over your company. She cannot understand that you might want to "get on with something else" because however glorious the game she is playing on the floor, she would never choose to go on with it rather than come up for a cuddle or share a joke. She cannot understand that there is a separate you, with a life and personality of your own, because there is not yet a separate her. You are her other half, her completion, and she has no concept of a world or an activity which is separate from her.

She will learn. In a year or so she will know that you and she are separate; that you have different likes and dislikes, different ideas about what should and shouldn't be done and different views of what is funny. She will have to learn, then, that it is *safe* to be separate; that while being an individual person in her own right may lead to quarrels, even quarrels do not spoil the love between you. But she is not ready for that yet. Right now she is learning *how* to love; practicing loving for the whole of her life. The more she can love you — and her other "special people" — and feel herself loved back, the more generously she will be able to give and take love when she grows up.

One day there may be grandchildren who will bask, as her babies, in all the warmth you are giving her now.

A NOTE ABOUT THE AUTHOR

Penelope Leach was educated at Cambridge University and the London School of Economics, where she received her Ph.D. in social psychology for a study of the effects of different kinds of upbringing and discipline on personality development. She has lectured at the London School of Economics on psychology and child development, and for four years ran a study, under the auspices of Britain's Medical Research Council, of the effects of babies on their parents. She is vice-president of the Pre-School Playgroups Association and the Health Visitors' Association, has served on the committee of the Developmental Section of the British Psychological Society, and is the author of *Your Baby & Child*, *Your Growing Child*, and *Babyhood*. She is married to an energy specialist, and they have two children.

A NOTE ON THE TYPE

The text of this book was set in Sabon, a type face designed by Jan Tschichold (1902–1974), the well-known German typographer. Because it was designed in Frankfurt, Sabon was named for the famous Frankfurt type founder Jacques Sabon, who died in 1580 while manager of the Egenolff foundry.

Based loosely on the original designs of Claude Garamond (c. 1480–1561), Sabon is unique in that it was explicitly designed for hot-metal composition on both the Monotype and Linotype machines as well as for film composition.